To:

From:

Jesus has a message just for you. It is whispered in every word of the New Testament:

If only you knew that I came to help and not judge. If only you knew that tomorrow will be better than today. If only you knew the gift that I bring you: eternal life. If only you knew I want you safely home with Me. *If only you knew.*

What wishful, wistful words to come from the lips of God. How kind that He would let us hear them. How important it is that we stop to hear them. If only we knew to trust God. Trust that He is in our corner. Trust that God wants what is best for us.

If only we could learn to trust Him. Won't you trust Him?

Read: JOHN 14:27

God wants to change your face. No, not the color of your eyes, or the shape of your nose, or whether or not you have dimples. God wants to add His glory to your face—just like He did for Moses. When Moses came down the mountain with the Ten Commandments, his face "was shining because he had talked with the Lord" (Exodus 34:29).

Let me be very clear. This change is *God's* job, not *yours*. Your job is not to stick some fake, frozen smile on your face. Your job is simply to stand before God with a prepared and willing heart and then let God change your face.

And He does. He wipes away the tears. He mops away the sweat. He softens your worried brow. He changes your face as you worship Him. God makes you shine.

Read: JOHN 17:10

January 1

You can talk to God because God listens. *Always.*

What you have to say matters in heaven. He takes you very seriously. Even if your words come out wrong... even if what you have to say doesn't seem important to anyone else, it's important to God, and He listens.

He listens in the morning and in the night... and even in math class. He listens to the joy of the ballplayer who makes the game-winning play... and to the tears of the one who didn't. He listens to the sadness of someone who is sick... and to the fears of someone facing the first day in a new school. When the lonely ask for a friend and the frightened ask for courage, God listens.

Read: PSALM 142:2

December 29

Friends are the people we go to for encouragement and a listening ear. But sometimes even our friends can hurt us. Maybe a friend has said something hurtful. Maybe a friend has betrayed you. Or maybe a friend has recently moved away.

A troubled friendship can leave you feeling empty and hurt inside. Jesus understands. After all, Judas was His friend, and Judas betrayed Him. Peter was His friend, and Peter said he didn't even know Him. John was His friend, and he ran away when Jesus was arrested.

Friends aren't always faithful, but God is. So the next time a troubled friendship leaves you hurt, ask God to comfort you. Ask Him to fill that emptiness with His peace. And then pray for your friend—God can touch the heart of your friend too.

Read: ACTS 1:14

Do you ever feel invisible? As if nobody even notices you? Learn to see yourself as God sees you—covered with the "clothes of salvation" and wrapped in "a coat of goodness" (Isaiah 61:10).

Do you ever feel like a nobody? When you do, remember what you're really worth. Remember what—or rather who—God gave to save you: "You were bought with the precious blood of the death of Christ, who was like a pure and perfect lamb" (1 Peter 1:19).

God *chooses* you to be His child. That can be hard to remember sometimes. So pray about it. Think about it. Let the way God sees you change the way you see yourself.

Read: 1 PETER 2:9

December 28

It's hard to believe that the perfect and holy God can forgive every mistake we make. Sometimes we get so caught up in thinking about how *bad* we've been, that we forget how *good* God is.

Of all God's creations, I think the snowflake is one of the best. Is there anything purer than a snowflake that's come straight down from the heavens?

Now listen to God's promises in Psalm 51:7: "Take away my sin, and I will be clean. Wash me, and I will be whiter than snow."

God promises to wash away your sins and to make you as pure and clean as that snowflake that's come down from heaven. Forgiveness is His gift to you—you just have to accept it.

And the more you accept God's forgiveness, the more likely you are to forgive others.

Read: 1 PETER 5:10

Do you ever worry? We all do.

Some worries can be fixed with a little studying or even a heart-to-heart talk. But what about those worries that are too big for you—like thunderstorms, or sickness, or the terrible things you see on the news? You could spend your whole life worrying!

Honestly, do you think that's what God wants? God didn't send Jesus to save you just so you could worry. Worrying can't fix anything, but God can. Trust Him with all those things you worry about. God has even "put His angels in charge of you" to "watch over you wherever you go" (Psalm 91:11).

Worry? I don't think so.

Read: PSALM 37:25

December 27

Have you ever wanted to do something so badly that you thought it would make you happy forever? Maybe you wanted to make the team, get a part in the play, or take a special vacation. Finally, you got to. And it was great!... For a while. But the happiness and joys of this world don't last forever. They aren't true joy. *True joy*—the forever kind—comes only from God.

True joy comes from admitting that there are some things you can't do—like forgive your own sins or save yourself.

It's kind of funny. In this world, admitting that you *can't* do something doesn't usually lead to joy. Confessing mistakes isn't ordinarily followed by total forgiveness. But then again, God is not known for being ordinary. And the joy that He wants to give you isn't ordinary either.

Read: PSALM 30:11

Have you ever done any decorating in your room? God loves to decorate too. Let Him live long enough in a heart, and it will begin to change. He'll move some forgiveness into that corner. He'll add some shelves and fill them up with His Word. It's not always pleasant though. You might feel uncomfortable when He knocks down that wall of jealousy or anger, but that new spirit of kindness He puts in will look and feel great. Then He'll paint your whole heart with love—love for Him and love for others.

God wants to give your heart a makeover. So He won't stop working until He's completely finished—until it looks just like *He* lives there.

Read: 1 JOHN 2:14

December 26

When you read about Jesus' life, it's as if He is saying, "Can anything make Me stop loving you? Look at Me! The Maker of all that you see. Watch Me sneeze, cough, and blow My nose. You wonder if I understand how you feel? See the toddler at Mary's table; that's God spilling His milk. Look into the eyes of that kid playing with His friends in Nazareth; that's God walking to school.

"Do you want to know how much I love you? Enough to leave heaven. To be a toddler and stub My toe as I learn to walk. To smash My thumb in the carpenter's shop. Enough to be insulted by the very people I created. To be betrayed by My friends. To die on the cross for you. That's how much I love you."

Read: ROMANS 5:8

January 5

Surprise! God does it again!

He answered a prayer. That's what He does for those who believe in Him, sometimes in the most surprising way! Look at what He did for these faithful folks....

When everyone said it was impossible, ninety-year-old Sarah had a baby (Genesis 17:17; 21:2). When no one else had the courage to try, David took down a giant with just a stone (1 Samuel 17:50). And even though it didn't make sense, Joshua marched around Jericho, and the walls came tumbling down (Joshua 6).

So don't *you* give up! Do you think you've got a problem too big for God? A test too hard? A fear too scary? A friendship too broken? Keep praying! God is watching. And He's already working on an answer to your prayers.

Read: GENESIS 18:14

December 25

On a starry night, more than two thousand years ago, Jesus was born. It all happened in a most amazing moment... a moment like no other.

The Holy One became a human. He stepped out of the majesty of heaven and into the arms of a humble peasant girl.

The All-Powerful One, in an instant, became flesh and blood. The One who was larger than the universe became the tiniest of infants. And He who created the world with a word chose to depend upon a young girl named Mary for His human life.

God had come down from heaven. God had come near to His people... to show us the way back home to heaven.

Read: PHILIPPIANS 2:7

God wants to be your home. He doesn't just want to be the friend's house, your clubhouse, your vacation spot, or even the place you hope to live someday when you're older. He wants to be the place where you live all the time—starting right now. The place that you come to for answers, for help, and for comfort. He wants to be your home.

Your Father wants you to live with Him all the time (Acts 17:28). God wants to be the home that you carry with you wherever you go.

Read: JOHN 14:23

December 24

You may be surprised to see some of the people in Jesus' family tree: Jacob the cheat, David the murderer, Rahab the pagan. It seems like Jesus' not-so-great-grandparents made some big mistakes.

Why did God use these people? He didn't have to. And why does God tell us their stories in the Bible?

Simple. He wants us to know that when people mess up and the world goes wild, God stays calm.

Want proof? In spite of all the mixed-up mess-ups of His ancestors, the last name on the list is the one He promised—Jesus.

No more names are listed after Jesus' name. No more are needed. It's as if God is telling us, "See, I did it. I sent a Savior for you. I sent My perfect Son to save My imperfect people. Just as I promised."

Read: MATTHEW 1:16

January 7

The Bible says that "those who are in Christ Jesus are not judged guilty" (Romans 8:1). It also says that God will "make right any person who has faith in Jesus" (3:26).

That is great news for God's children! Because sometimes, even when you *want* to do right, you do wrong. We all do. That's why God's promises are so wonderful! If you believe in Jesus and obey Him, God promises that your sins will all be taken away and hidden by Jesus. So when God looks at you, He doesn't see your sin; He sees the One who saves you—Jesus.

You don't have to worry about messing up. You've already won because Jesus saves you! Trusting in that promise gives you the courage to try to do the right thing—even when you know you might mess up. Trusting in that promise lets you be brave.

Read: HEBREWS 8:12

December 23

Did God have to give the birds a song and the mountains a peak? Was He forced to put stripes on the zebra? Why did He make creation so amazing? Why did He go to such trouble to give us such gifts?

You do the same thing. You hunch over a craft and bend over a drawing. There's glue on your fingers and glitter in your hair. But this isn't just any old gift. This is the extra-special gift for the extra-special person. Why do you do it? So your mom's eyes will shine. So your dad's jaw will drop. To hear those words of disbelief: "You did this for me?"

That's why. And that's why God did it. Next time you see a beautiful sunrise, just imagine God saying, "Do you like it? I did it just for you."

Read: 2 CORINTHIANS 9:15

January 8

In Bible times, the roads were often made of dirt, so people's feet were caked with mud. Washing those feet was a servant's job. But at the Last Supper, Jesus became the servant. He washed His followers' feet, the dirtiest part of them. And He will wash the dirtiest part of you... if you let Him.

Jesus will wash away that sin from your heart, if you will only *confess*—or tell Him—that you are dirty. Tell Him about that bad thought, that bad word, that thing you wish you hadn't done. If you pretend that you never mess up or sin, Jesus cannot wash you. You will never be clean until you first tell Him you are dirty. But if you tell Him, He will wash you "whiter than snow" (Psalm 51:7).

Read: JOHN 13:5

December 22

Have you ever traded for something? Maybe watched your mom and dad trade for a car? It usually goes something like this: *If you give me this, then I'll give you that.*

Other religions are that way. They are barter systems—which simply means people trade their way to heaven. Their god says to them, *If you do this for me, then I'll do this for you.* Their god saves them based on what they do (works), what they feel (emotions), or how much they know (knowledge).

Christianity isn't like that at all. We don't bargain with God. We don't have anything to bargain with. Yes, we should go to church, pray, read our Bible, and help others. But no matter how good we are, our goodness is never good enough to trade for His grace. His grace doesn't depend on what we do, what we feel, or what we know. His grace depends on Him.

Grace is His gift.

Read: PROVERBS 8:35

January 9

You might think, *Jesus, it's easy for You up there in heaven. You don't know how hard it is down here.* But the Bible says He "is able to understand" (Hebrews 4:15)!

Jesus knows, because He *Himself* left heaven and came to earth. He didn't send an angel or a messenger. And He didn't come as God. He made Himself completely human.

Do you ever feel angry, scared, or left out? Jesus did. He was once your age! He had parents to obey and brothers and sisters to get along with. He fell down, and fell asleep. He went to school and played with friends. He was laughed at and hurt. Jesus knows everything you're going through. It's one of the reasons He came to earth—so He would know what it feels like. So He could help you get through it.

Read: HEBREWS 4:15

December 21

The night Jesus was born was an ordinary night with ordinary sheep and shepherds. The night would have passed like any other—the sheep would've been forgotten, and the shepherds would've slept the night away.

But God loves to add His *extra* to the most *ordinary* of things.

So on that night, the black sky exploded with brightness. One minute the shepherds were sound asleep; the next they were staring into the face of an angel.

The night was no longer ordinary.

The angel came in the night because that is when lights are best seen and most needed. God shows Himself to us in our darkest times and in the most ordinary of things for the same reason. Because that's when He's most needed and best seen. He's easy to find—just look for the "extra" in the ordinary.

Read: LUKE 2:11

January 10

God uses your unhappiness to get your attention, to help you remember that heaven is your home. How sad it would be if you settled for earth when the joy of heaven is waiting.

You won't ever feel completely happy and at home on earth. You're not supposed to. First Peter 2:11 says, "You are like visitors and strangers in this world."

You see, God made you for heaven. Yes, you will have happy times here. You will catch glimpses of God's light. You will laugh and love and be loved. But those times are just a taste of what heaven will be like. In heaven, you will finally be home.

Read: JOHN 18:36

December 20

The truth cannot be avoided: saving ourselves simply does not work. There is no way to get ourselves to heaven.

But Paul told us that God has made a way for us to get to heaven. He gives it to us as a gift. That's right. A gift. Salvation—being with God in heaven forever—is His gift to us. For "every perfect gift is from God." And salvation is God's greatest, most perfect gift of all. We just have to accept it.

Write this down and remember it: Salvation is given by God, powered by God, and created by God. It's not something that we can earn. It's not something that God owes us because of the good things we have done. Salvation is God's gift to us.

Read: JAMES 1:17

January 11

Have you ever felt God with you? He's always with you. You won't see Him standing right next to you in line or sitting behind you on the bus. But He is there in different ways.

God is there in the kindness of a stranger, the beauty of the sunset, the hug just when you need it. Do you see Him now?

Through Jesus, God came to seek and save *you*. Even when you choose your selfishness over His love, He stays with you. He never forces you to believe in Him, but He also never leaves you. He goes with you wherever you go. He will use all His power to help you see that He really is God, that He loves you, and that you can trust Him to lead you home to heaven.

Read: LUKE 19:10

December 19

The city of Bethlehem, where Jesus was born, still exists today. If you visit the city, you can actually visit a small church there that marks the spot where some people believe Jesus was born. In the church is a high altar, and behind the altar is a little cavern lit by silver lamps.

You can go into the main building and admire the ancient church. You can also go into the quiet cave where a star set into the floor recognizes the birth of the King. There is just one thing, however. You have to stoop. The door is so low you can't go in standing up.

The same is true of Jesus. You can stand up tall to see the world, but to really see the Savior, you have to get down on your knees in prayer.

Read: JAMES 4:6

January 12

Martha was a friend of Jesus. But the Bible tells us about a time when she was worried. She was having Jesus over for dinner. She was *really* going to be serving God! She wanted everything to be just right. But she made one big mistake. She let her work become more important than her Lord.

Martha wanted Jesus to praise *her* for all her work. She forgot that she was supposed to be praising *Him* with her work. She forgot that the meal was to honor Jesus. What began as a way to serve Jesus turned into a way to serve herself.

It is important to serve Jesus. But don't serve Him just so others will see you, or so others will say nice things about you. Remember—you are the servant, and He is the One to be served.

Read: LUKE 10:40-42

December 18

Some of the saddest words on earth are "We don't have room for you."

Jesus was still in Mary's tummy when the innkeeper said, "We don't have room for You."

And when He was hung on the cross, the message was the same: "We don't have room for You in this world."

Today, Jesus is treated the same way. He goes from heart to heart, knocking and asking if He can come in.

Every so often, someone throws open the door of his or her heart and invites Him in. To that person Jesus gives this promise: "There are many rooms in My Father's house.... I am going there to prepare a place for you" (John 14:2). What a wonderful promise He gives! We make room for Him in our hearts, and He makes room for us in His house.

Read: REVELATION 3:20

January 13

In heaven, there is no difference between Sunday morning and Tuesday afternoon.

God wants to speak to you on the playground just as much as He does in church. He wants your praise in the lunchroom as well as the Sunday school room. He listens to you just as hard in math class as He does in Bible class. You may go days without thinking of Him, but He's always thinking of you.

Paul's goal was to "capture every thought and make it give up and obey Christ" (2 Corinthians 10:5). Make that your goal too. Think about good things, about God and His gifts.

Read: PHILIPPIANS 4:6

December 17

Can you imagine parents who want to adopt a child saying, "We'd like to adopt Johnny, but first we want to know a few things. Does he have a house to live in? Does he have money for college? Does he have a ride to school every morning and clothes to wear every day? Can he cook his own meals and wash his own clothes?"

No adoption agency would listen to such talk. The agent would hold up her hand and say, "Wait a minute. You don't understand. You don't adopt Johnny because of what he has. You adopt him because of what he needs. He needs a home."

The same is true with God. He doesn't give you His name because of your great sense of humor or your talents or your money. He doesn't adopt you because of what you have. He adopts you because of what you need—Him.

Read: JOHN 3:17

January 14

One of the greatest truths about God is that He loves you just the way you are... but He's still working on you. He wants you to be just like Jesus.

God cannot love you any more than He already does. If you think God would love you more if you never messed up, or never had any bad thoughts, you're wrong. If you think He would love you more if you made straight As... if you were taller, shorter, faster, smarter... you're wrong.

God's love isn't like the love of people. Some people may love you more if you are good or love you less if you mess up. But God loves you just the way you are. And because He loves you, He is still working on you. He wants you to be *just like Jesus*.

Read: **PHILIPPIANS 2:5**

December 16

I love Christmas cards. They are like promises printed on paper. Tiny bits of truth that appear in my mailbox. Line after line declares the reason we celebrate a birth that happened more than two thousand years ago.

Jesus became like us, so we could become like Him. Angels still sing, and the star still calls to us. He loves each one of us like there is only one of us to love.

Christmas cards are cheerful little reminders that say, "For God loved the world so much that He gave His only Son...so that whoever believes in Him may not be lost, but have eternal life"

(John 3:16).

Read: ISAIAH 9:6

January 15

Do you ever look around and see all the things you wish you had? All the things you don't have but your friends do? If so, then stop and just look at all the gifts God has given you:

- God sent His angels to take care of you, His Holy Spirit to live inside you, His church to help you, and His Word to guide you.
- Every time you speak, He listens. Every time you pray, He answers.
- He will give you the strength to do the right thing even when it is hard.
- He will always be there to comfort you and help wipe away your tears.
- He always wants to see you.

But the very best gift of all? You have been chosen by Christ. You are a beloved child of God!

Read: JAMES 1:17

December 15

Maybe you were hurt a long time ago, by a parent's blame; a teacher's words; a friend's betrayal.

Or maybe it was just last week. The one who owes you money just bought a new skateboard. Or you're not invited to the big party.

Part of you feels broken, and the other part is mad. Part of you wants to cry, and part of you wants to fight. There's a fire burning in your heart—the fire of anger.

And you have to decide: *Do I put the fire out or heat it up? Do I get over it or get even? Do I let my hurts heal, or do I let hurt turn into hate?*

Revenge is bad. But what it does to you is even worse. When you choose not to forgive, anger is all you'll have left.

Read: PROVERBS 15:9

January 16

God always answers your prayers. *Always*. Sometimes He says yes. Sometimes He says no. And sometimes He says... wait.

Waiting is hard. It's hard to wait for your turn. It's hard to wait for Christmas, and sometimes it's hard to wait for God. You may even start to think that He's not doing anything. But God is always working in your life. You may hear nothing, but He is speaking. With God there are no accidents. He uses everything that happens to bring you closer to Him.

Why does God ask you to wait? That's a tough question to answer, but God's timing *is* always perfect. And He will *always* do what is right for you.

So keep praying. God will give you just the right answer at just the right time. That's a promise!

Read: LUKE 18:7

December 14

When a shepherd looks at his sheep, he doesn't just see a large flock. The shepherd knows each of his sheep. Each one is special, unique. And he calls them by name.

When we see a crowd of people, we see just that—a crowd. We see people, not *each person*, but people. A herd of humans. A flock of faces. That's what we see.

But not so with Jesus, the Good Shepherd. He knows each of His sheep. Each face is special to Him. Each face is different. Each face has a story. Each face is a child. And each child has a name.

The Shepherd knows His sheep. He knows each one by name. The Shepherd knows you. He knows your name. And He will never forget it.

Read: JOHN 10:14

January 17

Does Jesus care what clothes you wear?

Yes! In fact, the Bible tells us exactly what kind of clothes God wants you to wear: "Clothe yourselves with the Lord Jesus Christ" (Romans 13:14). God's kind of clothing has nothing to do with jeans or shirts or dresses. It is your spiritual clothing that He cares about.

Listen to what Isaiah says about God's clothing: "The Lord has covered me with clothes of salvation. He has covered me with a coat of goodness" (Isaiah 61:10).

When you believe in God, He gives you a heavenly "coat of goodness" that is only for His children. You will never outgrow it, and it will never wear out.

God's "coat of goodness" is always a perfect fit.

Read: GALATIANS 3:26-27

December 13

My family and I once lived in Brazil. While we were there, we met several American families who had come there to adopt children. The families would spend days, sometimes weeks, struggling with a different language and a strange city. There were endless forms to fill out, dozens of people to meet with, and lots of money to be paid—all with the hope of taking a child home to the United States.

Hasn't God done the same for us? As Jesus, God came into our world, faced down the temple rulers, and paid the largest, most unimaginable price to adopt us. We have every legal right given to His children. We are just waiting for Him to return. We are, as Paul said, "waiting for God to finish making us his own children" (Romans 8:23).

Read: JOHN 1:12

January 18

Want to see a miracle? Plant a kind word in the heart of someone who is sad. Water it with a prayer and add a sunny smile—and then watch what happens.

Want to see some more miracles? Fix a snack for your mom or dad without being asked. Give a friend a pat on the back when she's had a tough day. Draw something special for a person who is sick. Bring in the mail or the newspaper for an older neighbor. Offer to clean up even when it's not your turn.

Sowing seeds of kindness is like sowing beans. You don't know how they grow or why; you just know they do. And somehow that one little seed of kindness that you plant will grow into a whole garden of good deeds.

Never doubt the power of a seed.

Read: HOSEA 10:12

December 12

It's fun to play hide-and-seek. But that's a game that God never plays. God never hides; He always seeks.

God started seeking right there in Genesis. He was in the garden, looking for Adam and Eve. They were hiding in the bushes, ashamed and afraid. Did God wait for them to come out? No, His words echoed through the garden: "Where are you?" (Genesis 3:9).

God knew where Adam and Eve were, but He wanted them to know He was searching for them. That He hadn't left them alone. He wanted them to come and find Him. All through the Bible God calls out to His children, hoping that they will come out and find Him.

He's calling to you too. He's not hard to find. He's only a word away. Pray that He will help you find Him today.

Read: PSALM 23:6

January 19

David wasn't perfect, but he did try his best to do the things that would please God. That is why he was called a man after God's own heart (Acts 13:22 NKJV). In Psalm 27:4, David said, "I ask only one thing from the Lord.... Let me live in the Lord's house all my life."

What is this "Lord's house" that David is talking about? Is he wishing for a building with four walls and a door to come and go through? No. The Bible says that God "does not live in temples that men build" (Acts 17:24).

When David says, "I will live in the house of the Lord forever" (Psalm 23:6), he's saying that he wants to live in the presence of God.

The wonderful news is that when you love Jesus, He promises to be with you wherever you go!

Read: MATTHEW 28:20

December 11

Do you want to know how to be better at praying? Just pray. Sunday school lessons about prayer are great, but to really get better at prayer, you have to—you guessed it—*pray*.

Whether you sit or stand, say them in your mind or with a shout—whether you are inside, outside, or even upside down isn't really important for your personal prayers. Do whatever works for you. But don't think about it too much. Don't be so worried about how your prayers should look and sound that you never get around to praying. Better to pray awkwardly than not at all.

God hears every prayer and blesses every person who prays. And the more you pray, the easier it will become. Soon it will be just like talking to an old friend—the very best Friend of all.

Read: JAMES 5:13

January 20

Can you imagine a world without any sin? It would be so much easier to be good! Why? Because the sin that is in the world can sometimes cause you to sin.

If someone pushes you, you might push back. Hearing other people grumble can lead you to grumble. Listening to the terrible stories on the news can make you worry. The selfishness in others can make you be selfish instead of sharing. It can make you walk away instead of stopping to help.

Because of sin, you've snapped at your best friend, argued with your brother or sister, and sassed your mom and dad. Sin breaks promises and breaks hearts. But in heaven all of this will end.

Can you imagine a world without sin? If so, then you can imagine heaven.

Read: ISAIAH 11:6

December 10

John's descriptions of the future in Revelation can take your breath away. Good clashes with evil. The pages are filled with the shrieks of dragons and blazing fires. But in the middle of the battlefield there is the most beautiful sight. John described it in chapter 21: "I saw the holy city coming down out of heaven from God. This holy city is the new Jerusalem. It was prepared like a bride dressed for her husband" (v. 2).

God pulled back the curtain and let John peek into heaven, into his future reward. And when John sat down to write about what he saw, he compared heaven to the most beautiful image earth has to offer. The holy city, John said, is like "a bride dressed for her husband."

We will never see anything as beautiful as God's heaven.

Read: JOHN 3:29

January 21

God knows that you aren't just like Jesus right now—but He's still working on you! Isn't that good news? You aren't stuck. You may be grumpy right now. But you don't have to live in "Grumpsville" forever. And just because you're selfish today, that doesn't mean you have to be selfish for your whole life.

Who said you can't change your heart? And why do people say things like "I have a bad temper. That's just the way I am"? Would you say that if something were wrong with your body? "I have a broken leg. That's just the way I am." Of course not! You would get help.

So can you get help for your selfishness or your grumpiness? Of course you can! Jesus can change your heart. He will help you have a heart just like His.

Read: ISAIAH 64:8

What if the only gift God ever gave you was His grace—His forgiveness so that you can go to heaven?

Maybe you've begged God to help you pass a test or heal your loved one. What if His answer is, "No. My grace is enough. Saving you is enough"? Would you be happy?

From heaven's point of view, grace *is* enough. If the only thing God did was save us, could we complain? If He gave us eternal life, would we dare grumble about sickness? If He gave us all the riches of heaven, would we whine about money?

If you have eyes to read these words and hands to turn this page, God has already given you a mountain of grace. But because He loves you so much, He doesn't just give you grace. He answers your prayers too.

Read: PHILIPPIANS 4:11

January 22

Jesus chose to come to earth in a human body... just like yours. The mouth that called Lazarus out of the grave was human... just like your mouth. The hand that touched the leper had dirt under its nails. And His tears came from a heart that was as broken as yours or mine has ever been.

Because Jesus was so human, people came to Him. My, how they came to Him. They came at night as Nicodemus did. They touched Him as He walked down the street. They followed Him around the sea. They invited Him into their homes and sat their children at His feet. Why? Because He refused to be an "I'm-better-than-you" superstar on a stage. Instead, He chose to be a real person who could be touched and known by people... just like you.

Read: PSALM 136:23

December 8

When we pray, we are telling God that we need Him. We are admitting that without Him, we know we would never make it to heaven. It's only by His mercy that we're lifted up and saved. Prayer reminds us of *who God is* (the One in charge) and *who we are* (the one He loves enough to help).

I believe there's great power in prayer. I believe God heals the sick and wounded and that He can raise the dead. But I don't believe we tell God what to do and when to do it.

God knows that sometimes we don't even know what we should pray for. When we trust our prayers to Him, we trust Him to do what's right for us—even if it's not what we asked for. We let God decide what is best.

Read: JAMES 5:16

January 23

You are invited to sit at God's table. Not because of how good you are, but because you believe God's promises to take His children home to heaven. You'll take your seat next to all the other sinners who've obeyed God and been washed clean of their sins—people like Moses and David and Ruth. And you will all share in God's glory and His blessings.

Here are just some of the blessings that will be waiting for you at His table: All your sins will be forgotten (Romans 8:1). You will be a part of God's kingdom (Colossians 1:13). You will be a child of God (Romans 8:15). You can go to God at any time (Ephesians 2:18). God will never leave you (Hebrews 13:5).

And… *these blessings will last forever* (1 Peter 1:4)!

Read: PSALM 23:5

December 7

You probably don't think much about death. But you probably do a lot to avoid it. You take vitamins, get your shots, look both ways before crossing the street. Why? Because you're worried about staying alive. That won't be a worry in heaven, because you'll live forever.

In fact, you won't worry at all. We won't worry about getting hurt in heaven, because in heaven we'll feel no pain. We won't worry about getting sick in heaven, because in heaven we'll be healthy forever.

On earth we are made of dust. Our physical bodies grow old and wear out. But in heaven our bodies will be different. They will never grow old or wear out. Jesus promises that if we will believe in Him, if we will "be faithful," then He will give us "the crown of life" (Revelation 2:10).

Read: REVELATION 21:4

January 24

Jesus had been teaching people for hours. He needed to get away from the crowds. He needed to rest and to relax with His friends. So He got in a boat and crossed over the Sea of Galilee.

But the people followed Him. When Jesus stepped out of the boat, He stepped into a sea of people. And Jesus felt sorry for them. His love for the people was greater than His need for rest.

Many of those He healed would never say, "Thank You," but He healed them anyway. Most just wanted to be healthy, not holy, but He healed them anyway. Some of those who asked for bread would cry for Him to be killed just a few months later, but He healed them anyway.

Jesus cared for them... anyway.

Read: MARK 6:34

December 6

Even Jesus didn't have a perfect family. Look at what He said: "My true brother and sister and mother are those who do the things God wants" (Mark 3:35).

When Jesus' brothers didn't share His beliefs, He didn't try to force them (John 7:1–9). He knew that His spiritual family could provide Him with what His own family didn't.

Maybe you don't have the perfect family, either. Where do you go for encouragement? God has an answer for that— your church family. They are your brothers and sisters in Christ. Turn to them when you need a little extra care, a hug or someone to simply listen.

Let God's family give you what you need. That's why God gave them to you. And remember, even if your family isn't the dream family, don't lose heart. God can change families.

Read: 2 CORINTHIANS 6:18

January 25

When you believe in Jesus, God not only forgives your sins, but He also adopts you. Through an amazing series of events, you go from being a hopeless sinner to a beloved child of God.

What does that mean? It means that when you mess up, when you do something that you know is wrong (and we all do sometimes!), you deserve to be punished. But God loves you so much that He created a plan to forgive you. That plan meant sending His own Son, Jesus, to die on the cross. Jesus was punished for your sins so that you don't have to be. You are forgiven! But the story doesn't end with God's forgiveness. It would be enough if God just forgave your sins, but He does more. He adopts you and gives you *His* name.

Read: ROMANS 8:16

December 5

God's thoughts are not anything like ours. Our thoughts aren't even in the same neighborhood.

We're thinking, *I want to have fun*. He's thinking, *I want you to know My Son*. We dream of raising our scores. He dreams of raising us up to heaven. We do everything to avoid hard times. God uses hard times to make our faith stronger. We say, "I want to have it all." God says, "My Son gave it all." We love earthly things that rust and break. God loves heavenly things that last forever. We're overjoyed by our victories. He's overjoyed by our confessions.

We look at the sports player with the million-dollar smile and say, "I want to be like him." God points to His Son—who suffered the cross to save you—and says, "I want you to be like Him."

Read: PSALM 92:5

"Lord, don't you care that my sister has left me alone to do all the work?" (Luke 10:40). Martha's life was busy. She needed a break.

"Martha, Martha, you are getting worried and upset about too many things," Jesus said to her. "Only one thing is important. Mary has chosen the right thing, and it will never be taken away from her" (Luke 10:41–42).

What had Mary chosen? She had chosen to sit at the feet of Christ. You see, God is more pleased with your quiet attention than with your whiny work. The heart behind your work—why you do it—matters more than what type of work you do. A bad attitude spoils the gift of your work for God. But a good attitude makes heaven smile.

Read: 2 THESSALONIANS 2:16

December 4

Sin does to a soul what scissors do to a flower. A cut stem separates a flower from its life source. At first, the flower is still pretty and strong. But soon the leaves start to wilt and the petals fall off. No matter what you do, the flower will never live again. Give it water, dirt, or food. But the flower is dead.

When you sin, it's like slowly cutting your soul off from God, and your soul starts to wither and die. The result of sin is not a bad day or mood, but a dead soul. The signs are easy to spot—lying lips and cursing mouths, feet that run to do evil and eyes that don't see God. But unlike the flower, the soul can be healed—through Jesus. All you have to do is ask.

Read: ROMANS 6:23

How long will God love you?

Not just on Easter when your shoes are shined and your hair is fixed. Not just when you're happy and kind. Not just then. Everybody loves you then.

But how will God feel about you when you snap at everyone around you? When you have hateful thoughts? When you sass your parents?

Can anything separate you from the love Jesus has for you?

God answered that question long before you even asked it—by lighting up the sky with a star, by waking the shepherds with the song of angels, and by sending His one and only Son to be born in a stable in Bethlehem—to save you.

By sending Jesus to live and die on earth, God said to all people, "You're something special. Nothing can keep Me from loving you."

Read: ROMANS 8:39

December 3

There's a story about a fellow who went to buy a singing parakeet. The man lived alone, and his house was too quiet. The store owner said he had just the bird.

The next day the man came home to a house full of music, but he soon discovered that the parakeet had only one leg. He felt cheated, so he called the store and complained.

"What do you want," the store owner asked, "a bird that can sing or a bird that can dance?"

God always answers our prayers, but sometimes not how we expect—like the man's one-legged bird. When that happens, we have to ask ourselves: *What do we really want*? Remember, God only wants the very best for you. So if His answer is not what you expect, maybe you need to *change* what you expect.

Read: PSALM 18:30

January 28

Everyone makes mistakes. When you do, it can sometimes be hard to confess your sins—even to God. Maybe you're embarrassed or ashamed. Maybe you look at the people around you and think that they're all perfect. That their faith is perfect. That they never mess up. So you're afraid to tell God that you've messed up.

If that sounds like you, look carefully at someone Jesus praised for her faith. It wasn't the perfect person. It wasn't the never-messes-up person. It was a poor, sick outcast—a woman who had been bleeding for twelve years. But she had faith. She had a hunch that Jesus *could* help her and a hope that He *would* help her.

Which, by the way, is a pretty good definition of faith. *A belief that He can help and a hope that He will.*

Read: MARK 5:34

December 2

Life is like a big race. On the sidelines, that's God cheering you on. At the finish line, that's God clapping. In the bleachers, that's Him shouting your name. Too tired to finish? He'll carry you. Too hopeless to keep going? He'll pick you up. God is *for* you.

If God had a calendar, your birthday would be circled. If He drove a car, your name would be on His bumper sticker.

"Can a woman forget the baby she nurses? Can she feel no kindness for the child she gave birth to?" God asks in Isaiah 49:15. Can you imagine your mom asking, "What is that kid's name?" Mothers stroke your hair, touch your face, sing your name over and over. Do mothers forget? No way. But "even if she could forget... I will not forget you," God promises (Isaiah 49:15).

Read: ZEPHANIAH 3:17

January 29

The heart of Jesus was pure. The Savior was adored by thousands, yet He was happy to live a simple life. He was surrounded by sinners, yet He never looked down on them. The people He created wanted to kill Him, but He forgave them before they even asked.

Listen to those who knew Him best. Peter and John traveled with Jesus for over three years. Peter described Jesus as a "pure and perfect lamb" (1 Peter 1:19). John said, "There is no sin in Christ" (1 John 3:5).

The disciples worried over how to feed the thousands of people, but Jesus thanked God for the problem. The disciples shouted with fear in the storm, but Jesus slept through it. Peter drew his sword to fight the soldiers, but Jesus lifted His hand to heal. Jesus' heart was at peace.

Read: JAMES 3:17

December 1

There is a lot that we don't know about heaven, but this we do know: the day Jesus comes back will be a day of reward. Those who were nobodies on earth will be somebodies in heaven. Those who never heard people cheer for them will hear the cheers of the angels. Those who missed the blessing of a father on earth will hear the blessing of their Father in heaven.

Those who were put down on earth will be lifted up in heaven. The forgotten will be remembered, the ignored will be welcomed, and the faithful will be honored.

In heaven, the winner's circle isn't just for the rich and famous. It's for a heaven full of God's children who "will receive the crown of life that God has promised to those who love Him" (James 1:12 NIV).

Read: EPHESIANS 6:8

January 30

The book of Matthew was first written in Greek. The Greek word for "felt sorry" is *splanchnizomai*. Since you probably haven't studied *splanchnizomai* in school, this word won't mean much to you. But what it means is "in the gut."

So when Matthew wrote that Jesus felt sorry for the people, he didn't mean that Jesus just felt a little sad for them. No, it is far more powerful. Matthew was saying that Jesus felt their hurt like a punch in the gut:

He felt the limp of the crippled.

He felt the hurt of the sick.

He felt the loneliness of the leper.

He felt the shame of the sinful.

And once Jesus felt their hurts, He couldn't help but heal their hurts.

Read: MATTHEW 14:14

November 30

There is no way our human minds can understand the love of God. How can He love *all* the people in the world? How can He forgive us when we keep messing up again and again?

For thousands of years, people have thought about and wondered about the love of our Father. How could Jesus love us enough to step down from the power and glory of heaven and be born as a baby to poor parents huddled in a stable? How could God love us enough to send His Son to die on the cross to save us?

How can you explain such love? What can you say to that kind of love? The only thing you can say is, "Lord, thank You, and I love You too."

Read: EPHESIANS 3:18

January 31

Gideon was hiding when the Lord came to him and told him to defeat the mighty forces of the Midianites. That's like God telling the smallest kid in school to stand up to the biggest bully. Or to use a flyswatter on a rattlesnake! "Y-y-you b-b-better get somebody else," we would say.

That's when God reminds us that He knows *we* can't do it. But He can. And to prove it, He gives us a gift—a spirit of peace. It's a peace that helps us do the right thing. God gave it to David after He showed him Goliath. God gave it to Jesus after He showed Him the cross.

God also gave it to Gideon. So Gideon gave the name to God. He built an altar and named it *Jehovah-shalom*, which means "The Lord Is Peace" (Judges 6:24).

Read: **PHILIPPIANS 4:7**

Sometimes it's hard to leave the past in the past. You messed up, did that thing you said you'd never do, flunked a test, failed your parents' trust. You've told God you're sorry. But still you can't seem to let it go. You keep remembering the mistake.

Hear this: Even if you've messed up, even if you've failed, even if everyone else has turned their back on you, Jesus will never turn away. He wants to take all your worries away— whether you're worried about the past or future.

But only you can let go of your worries. No one else can do it for you. Only you can give all your worries to the One who cares for you (1 Peter 5:7). Say a prayer today and ask God to take your worries away... and then let Him!

Read: PSALM 68:19

February 1

Like any garden, your heart has to be planted with seeds and cared for. Think of your thoughts as the seeds. Some thoughts grow into flowers. Others grow into weeds. If you plant seeds of hope, you will grow love and joy. But if you plant seeds of fear and anger, you will grow worry, jealousy, and even hate.

The proof is everywhere you look. Ever wonder how some people seem to see the good in everything and everyone? They are so patient, so cheerful, so forgiving. Could it be that they planted seeds of hope in their hearts, and now they are enjoying the harvest of goodness?

Ever wonder why other people have such a sour attitude? Why they always seem so grumpy or so sad? You would, too, if your heart were a garden of weeds and thorns.

Read: GALATIANS 6:7

November 28

God rewards those of us who *truly* seek Him. Not just those who know every memory verse but those who let His verses change their lives. Not just those who lead the prayers but those who trust God to answer their prayers. And not just those who sing every note perfectly but those who sing praises to Him with all their heart.

The heavenly reward goes to those who seek Jesus. And what is the heavenly reward? Nothing less than being like Jesus. "And as the Spirit of the Lord works within us, we become more and more like Him" (2 Corinthians 3:18 TLB).

Can you think of a greater gift than to be like Jesus? Jesus had no guilt. He had kindness for the sick and courage for the challenges. God wants you to be just like Jesus.

Read: JOHN 15:10

February 2

God became a baby. As Jesus, He came into a world filled with problems and sadness. "The Word became a man and lived among us.... The Word was full of grace and truth" (John 1:14).

The important word in this verse is *among*. He lived "*among* us." Jesus stepped down out of heaven and into the body of a tiny baby. He made His throne out of a manger and His royal court out of some cows. He took a common name—*Jesus* (which back then was as ordinary as the name *John* today)—and made it holy. He took common people and gave them His holiness. He became a friend of the sinner and a brother of the poor.

He could have lived over us or away from us. But He didn't. He chose to live *among* us.

Read: ZECHARIAH 2:10

Sheep aren't smart. They tend to wander into creeks for water. Their wool soaks up the water, gets heavy, and causes them to drown. They need a shepherd to lead them to "calm water" (Psalm 23:2).

Sheep cannot protect themselves. They need a shepherd with a "rod and... walking stick" to protect them (Psalm 23:4). Sheep have no sense of direction. They need someone to lead them "on paths that are right" (Psalm 23:3).

We need a shepherd too. Because we, too, have a habit of getting in trouble. Because we cannot defend ourselves against the evil lion—the devil. And because we sometimes lose our way in life. We need a Shepherd to care for us, to protect us, and to guide us. And we have one—Jesus! He knows each of His sheep by name. He knows *your* name.

Read: PSALM 23:1

February 3

Some of you have never won a prize in your life. Oh, maybe you got a ribbon at field day for participation. Maybe you even won a cheap toy at the balloon-pop game at the fair. But you've never won anything really big. You've watched the stars of this world carry home the trophies and the blue ribbons. All you have are "almosts" and "could-have-beens."

If that sounds like you, then you'll love this promise: "When Christ, the Head Shepherd, comes, you will get a crown. This crown will be glorious, and it will never lose its beauty" (1 Peter 5:4).

Your turn is coming! The world may not see how great you are, but your Father does. And sooner than you can imagine, you will be blessed by Him!

Read: REVELATION 3:11

Once there were a couple of farmers who couldn't get along with each other. A wide, deep ditch separated their two farms, but as a sign of their hatred for each other, each farmer built a fence on his side of the ditch to keep the other out.

In time, however, the daughter of one farmer met the son of the other, and the couple fell in love. They were determined not to be kept apart by the foolishness of their fathers. So they tore down the fence and used the wood to build a bridge across the ditch.

That's just what confession does. When you tell God your sins, you tear down the fence that separates you from Him. Confession, then, becomes the bridge over which you can walk back into God's arms.

Read: PSALM 32:5

February 4

When you are hurt, you need healing. And healing begins when you *do* something. You tell your mom. You get a Band-Aid. You go to the doctor.

When you sin, your heart is hurt and needs healing. And when your heart is hurt, you have to do something. Healing begins when you reach out to God, tell Him how sorry you are, and ask Him to forgive you.

God's help is always near, but He only gives it to those who ask for it. Nothing comes from doing nothing. God helps those who bravely reach out to Him and ask for help.

When Noah built the ark, lives were saved. When the soldiers marched, the walls of Jericho tumbled down. When Moses raised his staff, the sea parted. God always stops to help those who call on Him.

Read: PSALM 145:18

November 25

The stadium is packed. Everyone has come to see *him*. As soon as he walks in, the fans are on their feet. He steps up to the plate. The crowd roars. He swings, and the ball soars. Home run! Fans are still on their feet long after he crosses home plate.

Not everyone can be a home run king. For every million kids who dream of it, only one makes it. Most of us don't hit the big ball, wear the gold medal, or give the president's speech. And that's okay. In this world, only a few people win crowns.

In heaven, though, it's different. Heavenly rewards are not limited to a chosen few, but "to all those who have waited with love for Him to come again" (2 Timothy 4:8). That's much better than any earthly crown!

Read: MATTHEW 24:46

Jesus refused to let anything turn Him away from what He came to do. His heart was full of purpose—one purpose.

Jesus' goal was to save people from their sins. His whole life could be described with one sentence: "The Son of Man came to find lost people and save them" (Luke 19:10). But He was not so busy working toward His goal that He was unpleasant to be around.

Just the opposite! Children couldn't resist Jesus. He found beauty in the lilies and joy in worshiping God. When His followers saw problems, Jesus saw possibilities. He would spend days with crowds of sick people and still feel sorry for them. He lived in a world full of sin and anger and hatred. Yet He still saw enough beauty in people to die for their mistakes and for ours.

Read: MATTHEW 20:28

November 24

It may surprise you to know that Jesus had brothers and sisters. But He did. Mark wrote this about Jesus' family: "His mother is Mary. He is the brother of James, Joseph, Judas, and Simon. And His sisters are here with us" (Mark 6:3).

And Jesus' family was less than perfect. They were human, after all. Mark even told us that Jesus' family didn't always understand Him. Once, they even tried to stop His preaching and take Him home because "people were saying that Jesus was out of His mind" (Mark 3:21).

How do you think Jesus treated His family when they didn't agree with Him? The same way He treated all people. With kindness and patience, love and respect. And that's just how He wants you to treat your family—even when you don't understand one another.

Read: MARK 3:35

February 6

The questions that we ask show the things that we do not understand. Maybe you have questions such as these:

How can God be everywhere at one time? *God does not live in a body like yours, so He can do things that your body cannot do.*

How can God hear all the prayers of all the people? *Maybe His ears are different from yours.*

How can God be the Father, the Son, *and* the Holy Spirit— all at once? *Could it be that the natural laws of heaven are different from those of earth?*

If people down here on earth won't forgive me, how could God ever forgive me? *God is always able to forgive—to give you His grace—even when people can't or won't. He can always give you His grace because He invented it.*

Read: MARK 10:27

November 23

Some people will do anything to be in first place—even if it means using their words or actions to push others into last place. For people like that, doing their best is all about being number one.

Don't get me wrong. God wants you to do your best. He wants you to use the gifts and talents that He has given you in a way that pleases—and praises—Him. If you're an A+ student, use your gifts to help others learn. If you're a great third baseman, show others how to be a good sport by the way you win *and* lose. If you're a fabulous artist, use your art to remind people of the beauty of God all around them.

Just remember... use your words, gifts, and talents to honor God, not to get honor and glory for yourself.

Read: EPHESIANS 2:10

February 7

If you could ask God for just one thing, what would it be? David told us what he would ask: "Let me live in the Lord's house all my life. Let me see the Lord's beauty. Let me look around in His Temple. During danger He will keep me safe in His shelter. He will hide me in His Holy Tent" (Psalm 27:4–5).

David was talking about living in the *presence* of God. David wanted to be so close to God that His presence covered and protected him just like the walls of a house. David wasn't just asking for a visit with God. He didn't want to stop by for a chat or a glass of lemonade on the back porch. He wanted to move in with Him and have his own room... forever.

Read: PSALM 26:8

November 22

Sometimes the one thing you want is the one thing you can't have. Maybe it's that you want your best friend to stay and not move to another town. Or you want your grandmother's sickness to go away.

So you pray and wait.

No answer.

You pray and wait some more.

Still no answer.

What if God says no? What if God says, "not right now," or even just plain no? If God says no, what will you do? If God says, "I've given you My grace, and that is enough," will you be content?

Content. That's the word. Content means being at peace even if God gives you nothing more than what He already has given—His love, His mercy, and His grace.

Read: JOHN 6:35

February 8

Jesus knows how you feel. Do you ever feel worried about your schoolwork? Jesus knows how you feel. Does it seem that you've got more stuff to do than one child could ever possibly do? So did He. Do people seem to want you to do more and more? Jesus understands.

Have your feelings been hurt? Are you ever sad or frightened? Jesus knows all about that. Does it sometimes seem that even your family isn't paying attention to you? That your friends have turned against you? Jesus knows how you feel.

You are precious to Him. So precious that He became a human just like you so that you would come to Him.

When you have problems, He listens. When you hurt, He answers. When you question, He hears. He has been there.

Read: ISAIAH 53:4

Different Bible translations can help us better understand God's Word. The New International Version of the Bible writes Hebrews 11:6 this way: "God... rewards those who earnestly seek Him." But the New King James Version® says, "He is a rewarder of those who *diligently* seek Him."

Diligently—what a great word! It means "never give up, keep going no matter what." Be *diligent* in your search for Jesus. Stop searching the Internet and search for Jesus. Don't just read a book about Jesus. Read dozens of them, starting with the Bible.

Don't be satisfied with a once-a-week church lesson. Be like the heroes of the Bible and *diligently* search for Jesus each day. Worship Him as the wise men did. Invite Jesus into your house like Matthew. Climb a tree like Zacchaeus. Do whatever it takes to see Jesus.

Read: HEBREWS 11:6

February 9

Let's go back in history a couple of thousand years to Rome and a shabby little room surrounded by high walls. Inside there is an old man seated on the floor. His shoulders droop, and his head is balding. Chains are on his hands and feet.

This is the apostle Paul. He once followed the will of God wherever it would take him. Now he is stuck in a run-down house and chained to a Roman soldier.

Paul has every reason to whine and complain. But he isn't. Instead, Paul is writing a letter to the Philippians that is still known today as the letter of joy.

What did Paul have to be so joyful about? It's simple. Paul knew that the sufferings he had were "nothing compared to the great glory" that would be his in heaven (Romans 8:18).

Read: PHILIPPIANS 4:4

Do you ever feel like you're all alone? Do you wish there was someone you could turn to for encouragement, hope, courage? There is. Jesus.

Turn to Jesus and His love. When you feel like your friends have all left. When you've messed up and you're not sure how to make it right. Ask Jesus to take away your confusion and guilt. Ask Him to show you the right thing to do. And trust Him to love you and help you through the hard times.

Jesus wants you to turn to Him. He wants to be the most important in your life, the greatest love you'll ever know. He wants you to love Him so much that there's no room in your heart or life for sin. Ask Him to come and live in your heart. He won't say no.

Read: ROMANS 14:8

February 10

Before the farmer plants the seed, he gets the land ready. He removes the rocks and pulls out the stumps. He knows that seed grows better if the land is prepared.

Confession does for your soul what preparing the land does for the field. *Confession* is when you invite God to make the field of your heart ready for His fruit.

Your confession might sound something like this: "There is a big rock of selfishness over here, Father. And over there is a stump of jealousy. Its roots are long and deep. And may I show you this soil that's too dry and crusty for seeds?" And so the Father and the Son walk the field of your heart together, preparing your heart for God's holy fruit. Confession invites God to plant His love and grace in your heart.

Read: PSALM 103:12

God gives us His blessings because *He* is so great—not because we are.

Why is that important to know? So you won't lose hope. Look around. Doesn't it sometimes seem like there isn't enough food to feed all the hungry people? Like there aren't enough doctors to take care of all the sick? Like there aren't enough people to tell the world about Jesus?

So what do we do? Throw up our hands and walk away? Tell the world we can't help them?

No! We don't give up. We look up—to God. We trust Him. We believe when He says He will use our hands to do His work. Galatians 6:9 says, "We must not become tired of doing good. We will receive our harvest of eternal life [heaven] at the right time. We must not give up!"

Read: 2 TIMOTHY 2:13

February 11

Leo Tolstoy was a great Russian writer. He told a story of a time when he was walking down the street and passed a beggar. Tolstoy reached into his pocket to give the beggar some money, but his pocket was empty! Tolstoy turned to the man and said, "I'm sorry, my brother, but I have nothing to give you."

The beggar smiled and said, "You have given me more than I asked for. You have called me *brother*."

When you are surrounded by loving family and friends, a kind word may be just a crumb to you. But to those who are lonely and needing love, a kind word is like a feast.

Read: 1 JOHN 3:17

Imagine this: On one side of you stands the crowd. *On the other side is Jesus.*

The crowd is yelling, teasing, and criticizing Jesus. They want you to do the same. *On the other side stands Jesus. His face is bruised and swollen. His eye is black. But He's ready to keep His promise to save you.*

The crowd promises you all the fun and flash and fortune of this world. *Jesus promises to save you from this world and take you home to His.*

The crowd tells you that if you want to fit in, you must follow them. *Jesus says, "If you follow Me, you will stand out. But I will stand up for you."*

The crowd promises to please you. *Jesus promises to save you.* God asks you, "Which will you choose—the crowd or Jesus?"

Read: MARK 8:34

February 12

It's important to pray. But it's just as important to believe that God is in heaven and answers your prayers. If you're having trouble believing, spend some time looking at the sky. It shows the power and majesty of God! Every square yard of the sun gives off the power of more than 450 car engines. And yet our sun is just one small star out of the 100 billion stars that make up our Milky Way galaxy. Hold a dime in your fingers and stretch your arm toward the night sky. That dime blocks over 15 million stars from your view!

By showing us the heavens, it's as if Jesus is tapping you on the shoulder and saying, "Your Father made all of that, so you can believe that He can take care of you."

Read: PSALM 19:1

November 17

Some people are not who they should be. Instead of giving friendship and encouragement to those around them, they treat them unkindly. They make fun of others. Sometimes they pretend that others just aren't important enough for them to even notice. We call them bullies. God calls them lost.

So what do you do when the bullies are the popular kids everyone else wants to be like? Do you dare to be different? Do you dare to be the person God made you to be? Or do you just go along with the crowd?

It's your choice, but you don't have to make it alone. Jesus Himself said, "You can be sure that I will be with you always" (Matthew 28:20). *Always*. When the bullies laugh, when the in-crowd puts you in the out-crowd, Jesus will be there with you.

Read: ROMANS 8:4

February 13

Life is filled with excitement and wonder. Chase after it. Give it all you've got. Don't tell yourself you're too young to make a difference. David didn't start out as a king—he was a shepherd and the youngest in his family. Samuel was a boy when the Lord first spoke to him.

Jesus doesn't set an age limit on His workers. He never says, "When you're all grown up, come and follow Me." He says, "Follow me" (Matthew 9:9).

God has a plan for every day of your life—including this day. Ask Him to show you what it is. Take a chance. Dare to be different. Make a new friend. Try out for the team. Lead a song in Bible class. Volunteer to help. Sure, it could be risky. But you might just make a difference!

Read: LUKE 17:33

November 16

Maybe you have questions about who God is and what He does. You're not alone. Many of God's people had questions, worries, and doubts too.

Thomas doubted that Jesus had really risen from the dead. So did Jesus turn him away?

Moses worried about talking to Pharaoh and leading the Israelites. Did God tell him to just forget it and go back home to Midian?

Job lost his family, his herds, his health. But did God turn away from him?

After Paul became a believer, he was arrested and beaten. Did God leave him?

No. God never turns away someone with a sincere heart. Tough questions don't stump God. He wants to hear our questions. God never turns away the honest searcher. Go to God with your questions. You may not find all the answers, you'll know the One who does.

Read: JAMES 1:5

February 14

God will give everyone the praise he should get (1 Corinthians 4:5). Wow! What an incredible sentence!

God won't just praise "the best of them" or just "a few of them." God will praise *everyone*!

You won't be left out. In fact, when it comes to giving out praise, God doesn't give the job to someone else. Gabriel doesn't speak for God. Michael doesn't hand out the crowns. God Himself will praise His children.

And what's more, His praise is personal! Awards aren't given for a whole nation church, or a family at a time. The crowns of praise are given out one at a time. God Himself will look you in the eye and bless you with the words, "You did well. You are a good servant" (Matthew 25:23).

Nothing could be more amazing than that!

Read: 1 CORINTHIANS 4:5

November 15

What does it mean to be just like Jesus?

The world has never known a heart as pure as Jesus', a person as perfect. He always listened closely to His Father so that He never missed a heavenly whisper. His mercy was so great He never missed a chance to forgive. No lie came from His lips; no sin clouded His eyes. He helped when others turned away. He kept going when others quit.

Jesus is the perfect example for how every person should live. God urges you to keep your eyes upon Jesus. Focus your heart on Him, and make Him the center of your life.

Read: EPHESIANS 1:18

February 15

The greatest thing about Jesus was this: His heart was led by God. That means that His thoughts were always on how best to serve God. This shows us how close He was to His Father. Jesus said, "I am in the Father and the Father is in me" (John 14:11).

Jesus took His instructions from God. It was His habit to go to worship (Luke 4:16) and to memorize Scripture (v. 4).

Luke said that Jesus "often slipped away to other places to be alone so that he could pray" (5:16). This allowed Him to hear God speaking and leading Him. Jesus once returned from prayer and chose His disciples (6:12–13). After another time of prayer, Jesus told the disciples it was time to move to another city (Mark 1:38).

Jesus let Himself be led by God.

Read: JOHN 5:19

November 14

The reed. It's a slender and tall stalk of river grass. Yet it's so fragile, so easily bruised. What once stood so proud and strong can easily be knocked over at the edge of the water.

Sometimes we can be like bruised reeds. Maybe we stood so tall and so proud once, thinking life was just right. Then something happened. We were bruised by mean words, someone's anger, or a friend's betrayal.

The bruised reed. This world knows what to do with us when we're no longer standing up tall. This world wants to break us so that we can never stand up tall again.

But the Bible tells us that God won't do that. He has a special place for people who are bruised and tired. And God will help us stand up tall again.

Read: HEBREWS 10:35

February 16

God promises to give *holy joy* to His children. Not just everyday joy, but holy and everlasting joy. And He doesn't promise it just to the rich or the famous or the superstars. He promises it to the most unlikely people: those who know they have messed up and who beg for His forgiveness; those whose hearts are broken because of their sin; those who forgive others—even the people who have hurt them deeply; those who keep their thoughts always on God and His love; those who reach out to hurting people with the love of Jesus; and those who are treated badly, laughed at, and made fun of for doing the good work of Jesus.

It is to these people that God promises a special blessing. A heavenly blessing. A holy joy.

Read: MATTHEW 5:3

November 13

Worship is what happens when you are aware that the gift you've been given is far greater than anything you can give.

Worship is like the traveler who is lost in the desert. The one thing he wants more than anything is the one thing he can't find—water. So when he does finally find that pool of water, he just can't help but shout out his thankfulness.

Worship is the thank-you that just can't be quiet.

Sometimes people try to make a science out of worship, with rules for our songs and prayers. But worship isn't supposed to be about rules—it's supposed to be so much more.

Worship is the heart's thank-you... offered by the saved to the Savior, by the healed to the Healer, and by the delivered to the Deliverer.

Read: PSALM 106:1

It's a fact that you can write down: *you are what you see*. If you only see yourself—and what you want—then you will be just like the people Paul described in Philippians 3:19: "The way they live is leading them to destruction. Instead of serving God, they do whatever their bodies want. They do shameful things, and they are proud of it. They think only about earthly things."

God doesn't want you only to see yourself. He wants you to see Jesus and to imitate Him. Seeing Jesus—and doing what He would do—is what Christianity is all about. Christian service—like helping the poor and being a friend to the friendless—is imitating Jesus. To see His love and power and kindness, and then to imitate Him, is the greatest kind of faith.

Read: JOHN 13:15

November 12

Some secrets can be fun—like a secret surprise birthday party for someone you love.

Some secrets can be dangerous—like hiding the fact that someone is being bullied or hurt.

But some things we think are secrets—like sin—aren't really secrets at all.

Some people think they can hide their sins. And they may be able to hide them from other people. Mom may never know that word you said. Dad may never know who really broke the window. Your teacher may never find out who cheated on the test. But those sins aren't really secret. Because the One who matters most knows.

God sees your secret sins—and He is hoping that you won't keep them secret anymore.

Read: PROVERBS 28:13

Think about the earth. Scientists believe that the earth weighs about six sextillion tons. That's a six with *twenty-one zeros* after it!

The earth is tilted exactly twenty-one degrees. If it were tilted any more or less, the North and South Poles would melt. And even though the earth spins at the rate of one thousand miles per hour, not one of us tumbles off into outer space!

If God can hold up the sky like a curtain, do you think He can lead you through your life? If God is mighty enough to set the sun on fire, could it be that He is mighty enough to light your path? If He cares enough about Saturn to give it rings or Venus to make it sparkle, does He care enough about you to meet all your needs? Yes!

Read: MATTHEW 6:26

God has only one requirement for getting into heaven: that we be clothed with Christ. But what does that mean—*to be clothed with Christ*?

Listen to how Jesus described those who live in heaven: "Around the throne there were... 24 elders sitting on the 24 thrones. The elders were dressed in white, and they had golden crowns on their heads" (Revelation 4:4).

All are dressed in white. The saints. The elders. So how would you think Jesus is dressed? In white, right? No. "He is dressed in a robe dipped in blood" (Revelation 19:13).

Why is Jesus' robe not white? Why is His robe not spotless? Why is His robe dipped in blood? Paul said simply, "He changed places with us" (Galatians 3:13).

Jesus wore our coat of sin to the cross.

Read: REVELATION 7:14

February 19

A little boy fell out of bed. When his mom asked him what happened, he answered, "I don't know. I guess I stayed too close to where I got in."

It's easy to do the same thing with your faith. But just as you are growing taller and learning more in school, this is also the time to grow and learn in Christ. Start some habits of faith such as these:

- Pray every day—really talk to God and tell Him about your day.
- Read at least one verse of Scripture every day.
- Memorize a verse each week.
- Go to church and Bible study.
- Decide to do one good thing for someone else each day.

Don't make the mistake of the little boy. Don't stay too close to where you got in. Jump right in, and start growing your faith!

Read: HEBREWS 6:1

November 10

If you've ever wondered how God feels when you mess up, when you sin, frame the words of John 8:11 and hang them on your wall. Read them. Think about them. Remember them.

Or, better still, drop down on your knees. Ask God to come and hear your prayers as you tell Him about the mistake that you made, the wrong thing that you did. Tell Him how sorry you are and how ashamed.

And then listen. Listen very carefully. He's saying, "I don't judge you."

Hear His grace and forgiveness in the words of John 3:17–18, "God did not send His Son into the world to judge the world guilty, but to save the world through Him. He who believes in God's Son is not judged guilty."

That is God's message to you—you are not guilty.

Read: JOHN 8:11

February 20

A lot of Christians can tell you what Jesus said. They know the verses by heart. They can say all the right words and sing all the right songs. They can "talk the talk." But not nearly as many people can *do* what Jesus said. They have trouble when it comes time to "walk the walk"—to live like Jesus.

It's very easy to say, "Obey your parents." It's not so easy to stop playing and clean up your room. It's easy to say, "Forgive others." It's not so easy to forgive that friend who called you names. It's easy to say, "Love your enemies." It's not so easy to be kind to someone who has been unkind to you. But it is "walking the walk"—and it's what Jesus wants you to do.

Read: EPHESIANS 5:8

November 9

A parent's job is to help his children when they're hurt. Think about it. When your feelings are hurt, do your parents tell you how amazing you really are? When you've been hurt, do they help you feel better? When you are afraid, do they wait with you until you feel safe?

Parents are supposed to help their hurting children. But what if you are away from your parents, maybe at school? Or if your parents aren't the helping kind?

Then remember you have a heavenly Father who is always ready to help. When you are laughed at, hurt, or afraid, He is ready to comfort you. He will hold you until you're better, help you until you can live with the hurt, and stay with you when you're afraid of waking up and seeing the dark.

Always.

Read: 2 CORINTHIANS 1:4

February 21

Happiness on this earth is not real happiness. So beware of people who tell you that you can find perfect happiness here on earth. And don't listen to people who promise that happiness is in having the right friends, the right clothes, or the right house.

Imagine a perfect world. Whatever that means to you, imagine it. Does that mean peace? Then imagine the place where you feel safest. Does it mean perfect joy? Then imagine your greatest happiness. Whatever heaven means to you, imagine it. Get a good picture in your mind.

And then smile as God reminds you that "no one has ever imagined what God has prepared for those who love him" (1 Corinthians 2:9).

When it comes to heaven, you can't begin to imagine how wonderful it will be.

Read: JOHN 14:2

Heaven was not unknown to Jesus. As believers, you and I will live in heaven after our time on earth, but Jesus did just the opposite. He knew heaven *before* He came to earth. He knew what was waiting for Him when He returned. And knowing what was waiting for Him in heaven made Him able to bear the shame and suffering on earth.

"He accepted the shame of the cross as if it were nothing. He did this because of the joy that God put before Him" (Hebrews 12:2).

In His last moments on the cross, Jesus focused on the joy of heaven. He kept His eyes on the prize of returning to God. By focusing on the prize, He was able not only to finish the race but also to win it.

Read: HEBREWS 12:3

February 22

The differences between our hearts and Jesus' heart seem so huge. He is so good, and we mess up so much. How could we ever hope to have a heart like Jesus?

Are you ready for a surprise? God wants to give you a heart like Jesus. When you become a child of God, He will give you the heart of Jesus. One of the greatest promises of God is simply this: if you give your life to Jesus, He gives Himself to you. He will make your heart His home! Paul said it simply: "Christ [is] living in me" (Galatians 2:20).

Jesus will move into your heart and unpack His bag. And He is ready to change you "to be like Him" to bring "more and more glory" (2 Corinthians 3:18).

Read: 1 CORINTHIANS 2:16

God isn't bound by time. He sees all people, from all times, from all places. No matter where we are, God sees us—from the backwoods of Virginia to the business district of London. No matter who we are, He sees us—the Vikings and the astronauts, the cave dwellers and the kings. From the hut dwellers to the mansion dwellers. From Bible times to modern times, God saw each of us *before* we were born.

And He loves what He sees. Heart filled with emotion and overcome by pride, the Maker of the stars turns to us and says, "You are My child. I love you dearly. I know that someday you'll disobey Me, turn your back on Me, and walk away. But I want you to know, I've already given you a way to come back."

Read: 1 JOHN 4:19

February 23

Faith is believing that God is real and good. But faith is a choice. You must choose to believe that the God who created everything hasn't left it all—that He is still here and working. He still sends the light of His love to chase away the dark shadows of this world. And He still hears and answers your prayers.

Faith is believing that God will do what is right.

God says that the more hopeless things seem to be, the more He will help you. The greater your worries are, the harder you will pray. And the darker your troubles are, the greater your need for His light.

God's help is always near and always ready for you. But His help is only given to those who look for it.

Read: HEBREWS 11:1

November 6

Have you ever watched an old western movie where the bounty hunter chases the bad guy? The bounty hunter always travels alone. After all, who wants to risk getting on the bad side of a guy who gets even for a living?

More than once I've seen a person so eager to get even that he was about to explode. The whole time I was thinking, *I hope I never get on his bad list*. Best leave these bounty hunters alone—you never know when they'll lose their temper!

If you're out to get even, you'll never rest. Your enemy may never pay up. He may never apologize. No matter how right you are, you may never get justice. And if you do, will it be enough? Best to just forgive and let God take care of the rest.

Read: ROMANS 12:19

February 24

The word *holy* means "to separate." The word's meaning can be traced back to ancient times, when it meant "to cut." To be holy, then, is to be a cut above... better than the rest... extraordinary. That's God.

I'm not a great sailor, but I've been in a fishing boat enough times to know how to find land in a storm. You don't aim at another boat—it might float the wrong way. Don't stare at the waves—they're always moving. Set your sights on something that isn't moved by the wind—like a light on the shore—and go straight toward it.

When life is stormy, don't follow your friends—they might go the wrong way. Don't stare at your troubles—they're always moving. Set your sights on the One who never moves—God.

Read: PSALM 46:10

Scientists understand how storms are created. They can map out the solar systems, measure the depths of the oceans, and send signals to faraway planets. They've studied our world, and they're learning how it works.

And, for some people, this loss of mystery has led to the loss of majesty. The more they know about the world, the less they believe in God. That's strange, don't you think? Knowing how things work shouldn't erase the wonder. It should stir up the wonder.

Yet the more some people know about our world, the less they worship God. They are more impressed with our invention of the light bulb than with the One who created electricity. Rather than worship the Creator, they worship the creation (Romans 1:25). No wonder there is no wonder. They think they've got it all figured out.

Read: PSALM 8:3-4

February 25

In John 1:46, Nathanael asked a question that is still being asked today, over two thousand years later: *Can anything good come out of Nazareth*? Can Jesus be real? Just come and see. Come and see the changed lives: the sad who now have joy; the angry who are now at peace; the shamed who have been forgiven; the hurts that have been healed; the orphans who are hugged; and the prisoners who have been given hope.

Come and see the pierced hand of Jesus. Watch as He touches the most ordinary heart, wipes the tear from the dirtiest face, and forgives the ugliest sin.

Come and see. He welcomes everyone who looks for Him. He ignores no one. He fears no question. Come and see Jesus.

Read: JOHN 1:46

November 4

The writer of Hebrews compares the Christian's life to a race. This race isn't an easy jog, but a demanding, hard, sometimes *agonizing* race. It takes a huge effort to finish strong.

Unfortunately, many Christians don't finish the race. Maybe you've seen some who stop on the side of the trail of life. They used to be running, living their lives for Christ. There was a time when they kept up. But then they became tired. They never thought the race would be this tough.

Think about Jesus and the race He ran. Jesus' best work was His final work, and His strongest step was His last step to the cross. Our Lord is the best example of One who kept going. He could have quit. But He didn't. He finished the race. By His grace, you will too.

Read: HEBREWS 12:1

February 26

Have you noticed that God doesn't ask you to prove that you will put your time to good use? Have you noticed that God doesn't turn off your air supply when you mess up? Aren't you glad that God doesn't give you only the gifts that you remember to thank Him for?

God is good to you because God *is* good. That is who He is. He blesses you because of His goodness, not because you are worthy of it.

Someone once asked a friend of mine, "Why should we help the poor who don't even want to be Christians?" My friend simply answered, "God did."

Would God help those who don't love Him? Those who don't even want to know Him? Yes! He did it in the Bible, and He still does it every day for millions of people.

Read: PROVERBS 22:2

November 3

Once a man dared God to speak: "Burn the bush like you did for Moses, and I'll follow. Crumble the walls like you did for Joshua, and I'll fight. Stop the storm like you did on the Sea of Galilee, and I'll listen."

So the man sat and waited for God to speak. God heard the man, so God answered. He sent a fiery passion for building a church. He tore down a wall of sin. He stopped the storm in the soul.

And God waited for the man to speak. But because the man was looking at bushes instead of hearts, bricks instead of people, seas instead of souls, he decided God had done nothing.

Finally the man asked God, "Have You lost Your power?" And God looked at him and said, "Have you lost your hearing?"

Read: MATTHEW 7:8

February 27

God is working in your life. When you choose to believe in Him, He saves you with His grace. That means that when you break one of God's rules—whether it is not obeying your parents, telling a lie, or gossiping with a friend—you have sinned. That sin separates you from God, and that sin must be punished. But because God loves you so much and because He doesn't want to be separated from you, He chose to send Jesus to be punished instead of you. He chose to forgive you and forget your sins. That is grace.

As you think about grace and about all that God does for you, answer these questions: Who is doing the work, you or God? Who is active, you or God? Who is doing the saving, you or God? *God*!

Read: EPHESIANS 2:5

November 2

Sin put you in a prison. Sin locked you behind the bars of guilt and shame and lies and fear. Sin did nothing but chain you to a wall of misery. Then Jesus came and paid your bail to get you out of prison. He took your punishment and set you free. Jesus died, and when you choose to believe in Him, your old sinful self will die too. You'll be made new—and free.

But the only way to be set free from the prison of sin is to pay the price. In this case, the price is death. Someone has to die—either you or a heaven-sent substitute. You cannot leave prison until there is a death. But that death happened on the cross. And when Jesus died, sin lost its hold on you. You are free.

Read: JOHN 8:32

February 28

There are people who live only to make themselves happy. And because they've never seen God in person, they believe there's no life except the here and now. To them, nothing is real except what they can see. Nothing is important except their own happiness, and there is no Creator and no heaven.

These people say, "Who cares? I may be bad, but so what? What I do is my own business." They're more concerned with having fun than knowing the Father. They're so busy chasing after good times that they have no time for God.

Are they right? Is it okay to spend our days ignoring God and thinking only of ourselves? No! Paul told us in Romans 1 that when we ignore God, we lose more than church on Sundays. We lose the very reason we were created.

Read: ROMANS 1:21-22

November 1

Just as germs make our bodies sick, sin makes our souls sick. And when it comes to healing our own spiritual sickness, we might as well try to jump to the moon. We don't have what it takes to heal ourselves. Our only hope is that God will do for us what He did for the man at the pool of Bethesda—that He will step out of the temple and step into our world of hurt and helplessness. That *He* will heal us. Which is exactly what He has done.

I wish we would believe what Jesus tells us: When He says we're forgiven, let's let go of the guilt and shame. When He says we're valuable, let's believe Him. When He says He'll take care of our needs, let's stop worrying.

God is strongest when we are weakest.

Read: ROMANS 8:37

February 29

You can't always choose what happens in your day. But you can choose how you think about it and what you do about it.

Choose love. *Love God, and everything and everyone God loves.*

Choose joy. *Look for things to be happy about.*

Choose peace. *Forgive others because God forgives you.*

Choose patience. *Instead of being angry at having to wait, thank God for a time to pray.*

Choose kindness. *Be kind to everyone around you because God is kind to you.*

Choose goodness. *Do the right thing—even when it isn't easy.*

Choose faithfulness. *Keep your promises. Be a true friend.*

Choose gentleness. *Let the things you say build others up, not tear them down.*

Choose self-control. *When things don't go your way, remember God has a plan for your life.*

Read: GALATIANS 5:22–23

October 31

Someday, according to Christ, He will come back. In the blink of an eye, as fast as the lightning flashes from the east to the west, He will come back. And everyone will see Him—you will, I will. The earth will tremble, the sky will roar, and those who do not know Him will shudder in fear. But in that hour you will not be afraid, because you know Him.

And you know that He is coming to take you home.

Read: JOHN 14:3

March 1

Imagine being in heaven surrounded by all the other Christians who were saved. I wonder if Jesus might say these words to you: "I'm so proud that you let Me use you. Because of you, others are here today. Would you like to meet them?" And, one by one, they begin to step forward.

Like the grouchy old lady who lived next door. You didn't think you'd see her in heaven! "You never knew I was watching when you did kind things in the neighborhood," she says, "but I was. Because of you, I am here."

Before long, you and Jesus are surrounded by all the souls you've touched. Some you know, and some you don't. But you're so happy for each of them. And how wonderful to hear Jesus say, "I am so proud of your faith" (1 Thessalonians 2:19).

Read: 1 CORINTHIANS 2:9

October 30

Water must be wet. Fire must be hot. You can't take the wet out of water and still have water. You can't take the heat out of fire and still have fire.

In the same way, you can't take the love out of God and still have God. For He was and is... *love*.

Search deep within Him. Explore every corner of His Word. Peek into every angle. Love is all you will find. Go to the very beginning of Genesis, and you'll find it. Go to every story of every Bible hero, and you'll find it. Go all the way to the end of Revelation, and you'll see it.

Love.

No bitterness. No evil. No meanness. Just love. Perfect love. Never-ending love. Pure love. God is love.

Read: 1 JOHN 4:16

March 2

Do you want to make a difference in your world? Live a holy life. What does that mean? It means you choose to:

Obey your parents.

Be the one at school who refuses to cheat.

Be the neighbor who is helpful and kind.

Be the one who does the chores but never complains.

Be careful with your money and always give some to God.

Enjoy life and keep a smile on your face.

Live like Jesus, not just talk about Him.

People are watching the way you act more than they are listening to what you say. So although it's important to talk about Jesus and to share His Word, it's even more important to live like Jesus.

Read: MATTHEW 5:16

One night during family devotions, I set an empty plate in front of each of my daughters. In the center of the table, I placed a collection of fruit, raw vegetables, and Oreo cookies. "Every day," I explained, "God prepares for us a plate of experiences. What kind of plate do you most enjoy?"

Sarah put three cookies on her plate. Some days are like that, aren't they? "Three-cookie days." But many are not. Sometimes our plate has twenty-four hours of celery, carrots, and squash. God knows we need to build up our muscles. It may be hard to swallow, but isn't it for our own good? Most days, however, have a little bit of everything.

The next time your plate—er, day—has more "broccoli" than "Oreos," remember who made it. And talk to God about it. Jesus did.

Read: JEREMIAH 29:11

March 3

Jesus said, "When you pray, you should pray like this: 'Our Father in heaven, we pray that your name will always be kept holy. We pray that your kingdom will come'" (Matthew 6:9–10).

When you say, "We pray that your kingdom will come," you are inviting God Himself to walk into your world. To be the Lord of your life—your entire life. You want His will to rule in your heart. You want everything you say and do to be pleasing to Him. You want Him to guide your relationships with your family and friends, and to take charge of your doubts and fears.

This is no small prayer! Who are you to ask such a thing? Who are you to ask God to take control of your world? *You are His child*!

Read: HEBREWS 4:16

October 28

When we look at others, our eyes search for many things that just aren't important. Is he rich? Is she pretty? What color is his skin? Is she popular? These things don't matter to God. He sees two kinds of people: the saved and the lost.

From His point of view, every person is either:

• Entering through the narrow gate or the wide gate (Matthew 7:13–14).

• Called to heaven or headed for hell (Mark 16:15–16).

Ask God to help you see others the way He does. To have a heart like God's is to look into the faces of the saved and be happy. They're headed for heaven. To have a heart like God's is to look into the faces of the lost and pray. For unless they turn to God, they're headed for an eternity without Him.

Read: 2 CORINTHIANS 5:16

March 4

In Jesus' day, washing feet was a servant's job. But not just any servant, the lowest of all the servants. No one wanted the job of washing feet.

But at the Passover meal, the One with the towel and the bowl of water was Jesus. The King of the universe was the One kneeling at their feet. The hands that had shaped the stars now washed away filth. Fingers that had formed mountains now rubbed toes. One day all nations will bow down before Him, but on that day He bowed before His disciples.

Hours before His own death on the cross, Jesus thought of only one thing. He wanted His disciples to know how much He loved them. He wasn't just washing away dirt. He was washing away their doubts.

Read: LUKE 22:27

God's faithfulness to us has never depended on our faithfulness to Him. He's faithful even when we aren't. He keeps His promises even when we don't. He's made a habit of using people even when we don't think He can.

Need an example? The feeding of the five thousand. It's the only miracle—except those from Jesus' final week—that is written about in all four Gospels. Why did all four writers think it was worth telling? Maybe they wanted to show us how God doesn't give up even when His people do.

When the disciples didn't pray, Jesus prayed. When the disciples were weak, Jesus was strong. When the disciples had no faith, Jesus had faith.

God is greater than our weakness. In fact, I think it is our weakness that shows just how great God is.

Read: PHILIPPIANS 4:19

March 5

    As long as Jesus is just one of many choices, you probably won't choose Him. As long as you think you can handle all of your problems alone, you don't need a problem-fixer. As long as you are feeling happy, you don't need comfort. As long as you would rather follow your friends Monday through Saturday and follow Jesus only on Sunday, you're not really following Him at all. Because He wants all of you every day.

    But when you realize that you have sinned and your heart breaks because of your sins, Jesus will be waiting for you. When you're ready to give Him all your worries and cares, He'll be there. When your problems flash around you like lightning in a storm, Jesus will be right there in the middle of the storm—waiting to save you.

Read: MATTHEW 11:28

A lot of us live with a secret fear that God is angry at us. Somewhere, sometime, some Sunday school class or television show made us believe that God is just waiting for a chance to catch us being bad so that He can punish us.

Nothing could be more wrong! God cares for us and only wants to share His love with us.

We have a heavenly Father, filled with compassion—which means that when we hurt, He hurts. We serve a God who says that even when we're stressed out and feel like nothing is going right, He is waiting for us. He's ready to wrap us up in His love whether we win or lose.

God doesn't come forcing His way into anyone's heart. He comes into our hearts like a gentle lamb, not a roaring lion.

Read: 1 JOHN 4:18

March 6

What is a second chance? It's the teacher throwing away the failed test and saying, "I know you can do better." It's the friend you've hurt who says, "I forgive you." It's the parent who hugs you and says, "Let's try that again."

And it's the Savior who loves you so much that He died to save you.

You see, Jesus came for one reason: to give His life to save to save all of us. To give us a second chance. He loves each of us so much that He would have suffered through anything to save us. And He did.

Jesus—who was perfect and without any sin—gave His perfection to us. And all our sins, all our mistakes and imperfections, were given to Him. Because of Jesus, we are forgiven and given a second chance.

Read: 1 PETER 3:18

Have you been there? You knew right from wrong. And you chose wrong. Like you were standing on the edge of the cliff, trying to make a decision, when the ground of your goodness just gave way, and down you went. *Poof!*

Now what do you do? When you fall, you can forget it. You can fib about it. Or you can face it.

We can't keep secrets from God. Confession isn't telling God what we did. He already knows. Confession is simply agreeing with God that what we did was wrong.

How can God forgive if we don't admit our guilt? Ahh, there's that word: *guilt.* Isn't that what we want to avoid? But is guilt so bad? Guilt simply means that we know right from wrong, that we hope to do better next time.

Read: 2 CORINTHIANS 5:17

Look at Jonah in the belly of the fish. He's floating around with tummy juices and sucked-in seaweed. He prays. Before he can say amen, the belly rumbles, the fish belches, and Jonah lands face-first on the beach.

Look at Daniel in the lions' den, about to be swallowed.

Or look at Joseph in the pit, a dusty hole in a hot desert. Like Jonah and Daniel, Joseph is trapped. No exit. No hope. But even though Joseph's road to the palace takes a turn through a pit and a prison, he ends up at the throne.

The stories of the Bible often go this way. One close call after another. Just when the lion is about to pounce, just when the prison door clangs shut, Calvary comes—and God saves the day! Just in time.

Read: DANIEL 6:16

October 24

Why do Jesus and His angels rejoice over one sinner who repents? Can they see something we can't? Do they know something we don't? Yes! They know what heaven holds.

Heaven is filled with those people who let God change them. In heaven, all fighting will stop because jealousy won't exist. Gossips won't gather because there will be no secrets. Every sin is gone. Every fear is forgotten. Every worry is past.

Heaven is like pure wheat. No weeds. Pure gold. No other metals. Pure love. No selfishness. Pure hope. No fear. It's no surprise that the angels rejoice when one sinner repents. They know that one more Christian will join the wonders of heaven. They know what heaven holds.

Read: LUKE 15:10

March 8

You hear a lot of people talk about God and about Jesus. But when it comes to the Holy Spirit, nobody says much. And sometimes the thought of a "spirit" can be confusing, maybe even frightening.

The Holy Spirit is nothing to be afraid of—He is a gift from God. He is the presence of God living inside us, and He carries on the work of Jesus in our lives.

The Holy Spirit works in three ways: He helps our hearts by giving us the fruit of the Spirit (Galatians 5:22-24). He prays to God for us when we don't know what to say (Romans 8:26). And He pours God's love into our hearts (5:5).

The Holy Spirit is God living in you—and that is nothing to be frightened of!

Read: ROMANS 8:14

Think for a minute about this question: What if the Spirit of God weren't here on earth? If you think people can be mean now, imagine what we would be like without the presence of God! If you think we are hateful to each other now, imagine the world without the Holy Spirit. If you think there is loneliness and sadness and guilt now, imagine life without the touch of Jesus.

No forgiveness. No hope. No acts of kindness. No words of love. No more food given in His name. No more songs sung to His praise. No more good deeds done in His honor. If God took away His angels, His grace, His promise of eternal life, and His servants, what would the world be like?

In a word: empty. I'd much rather have a world full of Jesus.

Read: REVELATION 2:26

To pray "Your will be done" is to search for what God wants for you. The word *will* means "strong desire." So what *is* God's strong desire for your life? What is His heart's greatest hope? It's no secret. God's greatest desire is to save you. He has gone to a lot of trouble to show us His will. He gave His Son to lead us, His Word to teach us, and His Holy Spirit to guide us.

God is not the God of confusion or doubt. Wherever He sees someone who is truly seeking Him, whenever He knows someone's heart is filled with questions, God is there. And you can believe He is doing whatever it takes to help that person see His will. Because when you look for God, He lets you find Him.

Read: MATTHEW 6:10

Let's pretend there is a window in your heart. When you look through it, you can see God. Once upon a time that window was crystal clear. You could see God just as clearly as you could see a tree or a flower.

Then, suddenly, the window cracked. First one pebble hit it, and then another, and another. Those pebbles were the problems and worries that came into your life. Now the window of your heart is a spiderweb of cracks.

And suddenly God isn't so easy to see.

It can be frightening and confusing. Why would God allow this to happen? Why can't you see Him?

When you can't see God, trust Him. Because that is when Jesus is closer than you've ever dreamed.

Read: PSALM 138:7

March 10

There are many reasons God saves you. It brings glory to Him. It allows you to come to Him without any sin. It shows that He is Lord of all. But one of the sweetest reasons God saves you is because He is *fond* of you. He likes having you around. He thinks you are the best thing to come along since peanut butter.

If God had a refrigerator, your picture would be on it. If He had a wallet, your photo would be in it. He sends you flowers every spring and a sunrise every morning. Whenever you want to talk, He listens. God can live anywhere in the universe—the highest mountain or the most beautiful beach. But He chooses to live in your heart.

Face it, friend. God is crazy about you!

Read: MATTHEW 10:30

October 21

Faith is not believing that God will do what you *want*. Faith is believing that God will do what is *right*. God is always near and always there for you. Just waiting for you to reach out to Him in prayer and praise. So let Him know. Show Him your love.

- Write a letter to Him.
- Ask for His forgiveness.
- Be baptized.
- Feed a hungry person.
- Pray.
- Teach.
- Go and tell others about Him.

Do something that shows your faith. For faith that doesn't do anything is not faith at all. *God will answer you*. He has never turned away a true and genuine show of faith. Never.

Read: JAMES 2:26

When Jesus washed the disciples' feet, He knew the future of those feet. Not one of them would spend the next day following Him or defending Him. Those feet would run for cover at the first flash of a Roman sword.

So why did He stoop to wash the disciples' feet? The answer is in one word: *mercy*. Jesus knew what those men were about to do, and He wanted to give them something to remember—that He had washed their feet. He wanted them to know that those feet were still clean and that He had forgiven their sin before they even did it. He gave them mercy before they even asked for it.

That mercy is there for you too. When you choose to believe in Jesus and to obey Him, His mercy will make you clean.

Read: EPHESIANS 4:32

October 20

On the day God created humans, I wonder if He scooped and sculpted clay until a man lay lifeless on the ground.

I imagine the angels watching silently as God reached inside Himself, pulled out something, and placed it inside the man. It was the seed of choice. It would let the man—and all people after him—choose for themselves whether to follow God or not. No other creature in all the earth was given that choice.

God had given the man a part of Himself—that seed of choice. The Creator had created not just another creature but another creator. And the One who had chosen to love had created one who could love in return. Adam had a choice: to love God or turn away from Him.

And now it's your turn to choose to love God!

Read: DEUTERONOMY 30:19-20

March 12

Before Jesus comes into our lives, we may snap at our brothers and sisters or be selfish with our allowances. Maybe we are slow to obey our parents and teachers.

But then Jesus moves in, and things begin to change. The careless, mean words we throw around are thrown away. The selfishness that clutters up our hearts is cleaned out. Oh, we'll still mess up once in a while. But for the most part Jesus puts our lives in order.

Suddenly we find ourselves wanting to just do good. Paul says it this way: "In the past you were slaves to sin—sin controlled you. But thank God, you fully obeyed the things that were taught to you. You were made free from sin, and now you are slaves to goodness" (Romans 6:17–18).

Read: ROMANS 6:22

October 19

We all have to deal with the death of ones we love. God understands, and He wants to comfort you.

If you celebrate a birthday without a beloved grandparent... if a parent went to heaven too soon... if you're still missing a friend who passed away... God speaks to you.

God speaks to all who have stood or will stand near an open grave. And He gives us these words of comfort: "I want you to know what happens to a Christian when he dies so that when it happens, you will not be full of sorrow, as those are who have no hope. For since we believe that Jesus died and then came back to life again, we can also believe that when Jesus returns, God will bring back with Him all the Christians who have died" (1 Thessalonians 4:13-14 TLB).

Read: ISAIAH 49:13

God doesn't just give us the things we ask Him for—like good health and help with family and school. God also gives us what we need—a Savior.

And that's a good thing. For who would ever dare to say, "God, would You please take away my sins and mistakes by hanging Yourself from a cross?" Who would dare to add, "And then could You prepare a place in Your house for me to live forever?"

And if that weren't enough, would you ask, "Would You please live in my heart protect and guide and bless me with more than I could ever imagine or deserve?" Honestly, would we have the nerve to ask for that?

Jesus already knows the price of forgiving us. He already knows the cost of grace. But He gives us His grace anyway.

Read: LUKE 12:31

October 18

When God smiles and says we're saved, if only we'd salute Him, thank Him, and live like those who have just been given a gift from the commander in chief.

We don't usually do that, though. Instead, we keep trying to earn our way to heaven. Maybe we're afraid to admit that we can't do it on our own. That we aren't perfect. We'd rather impress God with all the great things we do instead of telling God how great He is. We make up extra rules and try extra hard. And we think that all of our hard work will make God smile.

But it doesn't.

God's smile is not for the one who brags that he did it all on his own. God's smile is for the one who brags that God did it all for him.

Read: DANIEL 9:18

March 14

In the fight for you, the devil may land a punch or two. He may even win a few rounds. But he never wins the whole fight. Why? Because Jesus sticks up for you. Jesus is "always able to save those who come to God through Him. He can do this, because He always lives, ready to help those who come before God" (Hebrews 7:25).

Jesus, at this very second, is protecting you. When the devil comes to tempt you to do wrong, Jesus helps you to stand strong against the devil. And He will "not let you be tempted more than you can stand. But when you are tempted, God will also give you a way to escape that temptation. Then you will be able to stand it" (1 Corinthians 10:13).

Jesus is on your side.

Read: ROMANS 8:34

October 17

According to Jesus, the things we do on earth matter in heaven. And they don't just *matter*. The things we do on earth *cause* things to happen in heaven. Help someone in need, and Jesus smiles. Sing God's praises, and the angels hum along. A child calls out in prayer, and the Father bends to listen. And, most important, a sinner is saved and everything stops—all of heaven celebrates.

We aren't always that happy, are we? When you hear about someone becoming a Christian, do you stop everything and celebrate? Is your good day made better or your bad day turned around? Maybe the news makes you happy—but do you celebrate?

When someone becomes a Christian, the heart of Jesus explodes with joy like fireworks on the Fourth of July. Shouldn't our hearts do the same?

Read: LUKE 10:20

After Jesus rose from the grave, He appeared to two of His disciples. At first, they didn't know Him, but when they "saw who He was, He disappeared. They said to each other, 'When Jesus talked to us on the road, it felt like a fire burning in us'" (Luke 24:31–32).

Don't you love that verse? The disciples knew they had been with Jesus because of the fire inside them. This isn't a fireplace kind of fire. It's a spiritual fire. God shows us His will for our lives by touching our hearts with spiritual fire.

He gave Jeremiah a spiritual fire for preaching. He gave Nehemiah a fire for rebuilding Jerusalem. And Jesus comes to set your heart on fire! He burns away sin and lights up the path for you to follow.

Read: LUKE 24:27

October 16

The Bible has been banned, burned, made fun of, and laughed at. Scholars have called it foolish. Kings have made it illegal. A thousand times over the Bible has been declared dead, but somehow it never stays in the grave. It is the single most popular book in all of history—the best-selling book in the world for years!

There's no way to explain it, which is perhaps the only way to explain it. The answer for the Bible's survival is not found on earth; it's found in heaven. The Bible is God's voice. It cannot be silenced.

The purpose of the Bible is to tell the world of God's plan and passion to save His children. That's the reason for its survival. It's the treasure map that leads us to God's greatest treasure—eternal life with Him in heaven.

Read: JOHN 1:1

March 16

There is never a place where Jesus isn't there. *Never*. There is never a room so dark that your greatest Friend is not around. He is always present, always seeking, always tender. It's as if He is gently tapping on the door of your heart—just waiting to be invited in.

Not many people hear His voice. Even fewer people open the door of their hearts to Him. But that doesn't mean He isn't there. He promised He always would be: "You can be sure that I will be with you always. I will continue with you until the end of the world" (Matthew 28:20).

Open up your Bible and listen for Jesus' voice. His Word will speak to you... if you will listen.

Read: HEBREWS 13:5

October 15

Don't ever think you're separated from God, with Him at the top of a great ladder and you at the bottom. God isn't up on Neptune while you're down here on earth. Because "God is Spirit" (John 4:24), He's next to you: God Himself is the roof over your head and the walls that protect you.

Moses knew this. "Lord," he prayed, "you have been our home since the beginning" (Psalm 90:1). Wow! God is your home. Home is where you can kick off your shoes and eat pickles and not worry about sitting around in your jammies.

Home is the place you know. You can know God just as well. You can learn where to run for rest, protection, and guidance. Just as your earthly house is your safe place, so God is your safe place of peace.

Read: JOHN 4:24

March 17

Jesus swapped the royalty of heaven for the poorness and hardship of earth for us. Sometimes He slept on borrowed blankets; sometimes it was the hard earth. He depended on the handouts of others. He was sometimes so hungry that He would eat raw grain from the fields or pick fruit off a tree. He knew what it meant to be homeless. He was laughed at. His neighbors tried to kill Him. Some called Him crazy. Sometimes even His friends turned against Him.

He was arrested for a crime that He didn't do. People were hired to lie about it. The jury had their minds made up before He was even arrested. And the judge ordered Him to His death.

They killed Jesus. And why? Because He came to give us a gift that only He could give—salvation.

Read: PHILIPPIANS 3:10

October 14

You may be a good kid. You may do your chores and your homework, and go to sleep without guilt. But apart from Christ, you are not holy. And if you're not holy, how can you get to heaven?

Believe. The work has already been done for you—Jesus did the work on the cross.

Believe in the goodness of Jesus. Believe that you can never earn your way to heaven with your own goodness. Let Jesus give you His goodness instead.

Is it really that easy? you ask. There was nothing easy about it. The cross was heavy, Jesus' blood was real, and the price was costly! You and I could never have paid it, so Jesus paid it for us. Call it simple. But don't ever call it easy.

Call it what it is. Call it *grace.*

Read: TITUS 3:7

Do you ever wonder where the power of God is? Maybe you've been trying to work out a problem—to get rid of a bad habit or a sin—and it just isn't working. Be patient. God is using today's troubles to make you stronger for tomorrow. He is *training* you. The same God who is making you grow taller will help your spirit grow stronger.

Do what is right this week. No matter what problems come your way, just do what's right. Maybe no one else is, but *you* do what's right. *You* tell the truth. *You* take a stand against evil. *You* be helpful. After all, even when you mess up, God still does what is right—He keeps His promise to save you with His grace.

Read: 1 JOHN 5:4

October 13

Jesus says our choices are clear.

On one side a voice whispers worries in your ear. It tells you to stay home and stay safe. You can't lose if you don't try, right? You can't fall if you don't take a stand, right? You can't lose your balance if you never climb, right? So don't try it. Just stay home, snuggle under a blanket, and stay warm and dry.

And there is the voice of adventure—God's adventure. It whispers, *Follow Me. I've got the most amazing adventure planned for you in My kingdom. There are hearts to touch, souls to save, songs to sing, prayers to pray—and you can be part of it all.*

Don't just hide under the blankets and stay home. Choose adventure. Follow God. Make a difference. Be His light in this world!

Read: PSALM 27:1

John told us that the blood of Jesus "*is making* us clean from every sin." That means, He *is always making* us clean. This cleansing is not just a promise for someday in the future. It is a fact for right now.

Jesus kneels down and looks at the most terrible things we have ever said and done. But He doesn't step back in horror. Instead, He reaches out in kindness and says, "I can clean that if you want." And from the bowl of His grace, He scoops out a handful of mercy and washes away our sin.

Because Jesus lives in us, you and I can do the same. Because He has forgiven us, we can forgive others.

Read: 1 JOHN 1:7

To know God as Lord is to know that He is Ruler and King of all the universe. To accept Him as Savior is to accept His gift of salvation that He offered through Jesus on the cross. To see Him as Father is to go a step further. A father should be the one in your life who provides for you and protects you. Earthly fathers sometimes fail at this, but God does not. See what He has done for you:

He has taken care of all your needs (Matthew 6:25–34).

He has protected you from harm (Psalm 139:5).

He has adopted you as His own child (Ephesians 1:5).

And He has given you His name (1 John 3:1).

God has proven Himself to be a faithful Father. Now it is up to us to be trusting children.

Read: DEUTERONOMY 32:4

March 20

The many different religions in the world believe one of two things—they either need God or they don't. They either earn their salvation by doing good things, or it is a gift from God.

People who believe they can save themselves are called *legalists*. They believe you can work your way to heaven if you look right, say the right thing, and belong to the right group. The power to save doesn't come from God; it comes from you.

These people look great on the outside. But look closely. Something is missing. *Joy.* What is there instead? *Fear.* They're afraid they won't work hard enough, be good enough, or do enough good. They're afraid they will fail.

But you don't have to be afraid. Because getting to heaven isn't up to you. It is a gift from God.

Read: COLOSSIANS 2:13-14

Some say Judas was a good man with a bad plan. I don't believe that. The Bible says, "Judas... was a thief " (John 12:6). Somehow he was able to live beside Jesus, to be part of the miracles, and still be unchanged. In the end, he sold Jesus for thirty pieces of silver. Judas was a rat, a cheat, and a bum. How could anyone see him any other way?

Somehow Jesus did. Only inches from the face of His betrayer, Jesus looked at Judas and said, "Friend, do the thing you came to do" (Matthew 26:50). I can't imagine what Jesus saw in Judas that was worthy of being called *friend*. But Jesus doesn't lie, and He saw something good in a very bad man.

Jesus can help us to see the good in those who hurt us too.

Read: ROMANS 12:14

March 21

When a friend came to Jesus and told Him that Lazarus was sick, he said, "Lord, the one You love is sick" (John 11:3).

The man didn't say, "The one *who loves You* is sick." No. He reminded Jesus of His perfect love for Lazarus. He said, "The one *You love* is sick."

When you talk to Jesus in prayer, the power of the prayer is not in you, the one who says the prayer. The power is in the One who hears the prayer.

So when you pray, you can use the same words as Lazarus's friend: "The one You love is sick... tired... sad... hungry... lonely... afraid." You can pray this way, because *you* are the one Jesus loves.

The words of your prayers may change, but what Jesus does never changes. Your Savior never misses a word. He hears your prayer.

Read: PSALM 34:17

October 10

What kind of people should we be? Peter told us, "You should live holy lives and serve God. You should wait for the day of God and look forward to its coming" (2 Peter 3:11–12).

The hope of heaven doesn't give us the right to do whatever we want, though. We should be holy and wait for the Lord.

We wait—in line, in class, in the car—*expecting* our wait to end. But how are we waiting for Jesus? Are we expecting our wait for Him to end? Are we looking for Him? Too often we are content to just wait, and we forget to *expect*. We don't let the Holy Spirit change our plans. We don't let Him lead us to worship so that we might see Jesus. We are waiting, but we are not expecting.

Read: 2 PETER 3:10–11

March 22

Do you ever wonder about some of the things that happen in the world? Do you wonder about things like starving children, Christians with cancer, and why bad things happen?

Those are tough questions. They are probably a lot like what the disciples must have asked when they were in the middle of the sea during a storm: "Jesus, don't You care?"

All they could see were black skies and waves as they bounced in their boat. Then a figure came to them, walking on the water. It wasn't what they expected, so they almost missed seeing the answer to their prayers.

Unless you look and listen closely, you might make the same mistake. God's answers are like the stars in the sky—there are billions of them. But some of them you just can't see yet.

Read: 1 TIMOTHY 2:1

October 9

You probably have a nice, warm house for your body to live in. Maybe even your own room. But have you thought about your soul's house? Is it warm and safe with God? Or is it left out in the world, where the night winds blow and the rain soaks it through? A soul left out in the world soon becomes cold.

It doesn't have to be this way. It's not God's plan for your soul to wander around in the world. God wants you to move in *with Him*. Under His roof, there is plenty of room. At His table, a plate is already set for you. In His living room, a cozy chair is waiting for you. Why would He want to share His home with you?

Simple. He's your Father.

Read: PSALM 91:1

March 23

"While Jesus lived on earth, He asked God for help. He prayed with loud cries and tears to the One who could save Him from death" (Hebrews 5:7).

Just imagine... Jesus is praying in the garden only hours before His death. Jesus is in pain. Jesus is filled with fear. At this moment, perhaps more than any other, Jesus knows how weak and frail His human body is.

The next time you are really sad, remember Jesus in the garden. When you think no one understands how much you are hurting, read this verse again. When you are feeling sorry for yourself, kneel down just as Jesus did in the garden. And when you wonder if God really understands how hard it is to live on this earth, think of Jesus' pleading prayer in the garden.

Read: MARK 14:33

October 8

Take a moment and offer these praises to God:
You are a great God.
You are holy.
Your truth never changes.
Your strength never ends.
Your discipline is fair.
You take care of our needs.
You light our path and show us the way to go.
You wash away our sins.
Your timing is perfect—never too early or too late.
You sent Your Son to save us, and at just the right time, He will come back again.
Your plan is perfect.
Sometimes puzzling and hard to understand.
But perfect.

Read: HEBREWS 13:15

March 24

To get into heaven, you have to be holy. You have to be perfect to live with God for all eternity. We wish it weren't so. We act like those who try hard will get into heaven. We pretend that we're good if we don't do anything too terrible. And we hope that our goodness is enough to get us into heaven.

That may sound right to us. But God says, "You must be perfect, just as your Father in heaven is perfect" (Matthew 5:48).

In God's plan, we can't compare ourselves to others. They are just as messed up as we are. The goal is to be like God— perfect. Anything else is just not good enough. Thankfully, God knows that we can't be perfect. So He sent His Son to be perfect for us.

Read: HEBREWS 10:10

As we get older, our vision of heaven should get clearer. Those who have spent their lives looking for heaven get a little excited as the time draws near for them to leave this earth. They get a little skip in their step as the Holy City comes into view.

After the artist Michelangelo died, someone found a piece of paper in his studio. On it, he had written a note to his apprentice. In the handwriting of his old age, the great artist wrote, "Draw, Antonio, draw, and do not waste time."

When you are young, time seems endless. There are so many years ahead of you. But time slips away quickly when you aren't looking. God has work for you to do here on earth—even as a child. So don't waste a minute.

Read: GALATIANS 6:16

March 25

God doesn't keep secrets from us. He told us there would be troubles. Just as Dorothy faced dark forests, twisted roads, and wicked witches on her way to Oz, so we will have troubles on our way to heaven. We should not be surprised by these things, because the devil lives in this world. But just because the devil swoops in like the wicked witch and laughs his evil laugh, we shouldn't panic.

Jesus said, "It is finished" (John 19:30). The battle is over. Keep on the lookout for the devil's tricks, but don't be alarmed. Jesus has already written this book, and He wins in the end. Satan may still play his evil tricks, but only for a little while. Just a few more twists and turns in the yellow brick road, and his story will end.

Read: JOHN 16:33

Just as you want to know that your parents are safe while you're at school, we all want to know what happens to those we love when they die. We want to know: *When we die, do our souls go straight to heaven to be with God*? According to the Bible, that *is* true! The Bible doesn't have a lot to say about the time between a person's physical death and being raised to live with God. It doesn't shout out its answers. It whispers them. And at the place where all those whispers come together, we can hear God's voice.

God tells us that, at death, the Christian joins Him in an instant. One moment he is on earth, and the next he is face-to-face with the Father. And it all happens in the blink of an eye.

Read: PHILIPPIANS 1:21

March 26

God's touch is a powerful thing! Have you felt it? It's a bit different from your touch or mine. It's the teacher who dried your tears or the friendly hug just when you needed it most. It's the nurse who holds your hand when you get a shot or the friendly face that greets you on your first day in a new class.

Can you offer God's touch to someone? Maybe you already do. Your hands pray for the sick, help bake cookies for the shut-ins, and hug the lonely. You have learned the power of a touch.

Or maybe you've never tried to touch others. Your heart is good, but you've forgotten how important one touch can be. Just look at how Jesus reached out to touch others. Aren't you glad He reached out to touch you?

Read: MATTHEW 8:3

Peter is standing helpless in a boat in the middle of a terrible storm. He sees Jesus walking on the water. Peter knows Jesus can save him. He calls to Jesus and steps out of the boat. But Peter begins to sink, so he begs for help. He hears his Savior's voice. Jesus catches him, and he is saved.

That is faith. Faith is knowing we can't save ourselves. It's knowing that all our good deeds won't keep us from sinking in sin. Faith is praying that Jesus will save us—and trusting that He really will. Paul wrote about this kind of faith: "You have been saved by grace because you believe. You did not save yourselves. It was a gift from God. You cannot brag that you are saved by the work you have done" (Ephesians 2:8–9).

Read: MATTHEW 14:30-31

God promises to take care of your needs.

The writer of Hebrews prayed that "the God of peace will give you every good thing you need so that you can do what He wants" (13:20). If you think about it, you'll see that prayer has already been answered in your life. Don't you always have bread to eat? You may not have everything you *want*, but don't you have everything you truly need?

After all, how can you complete the mission He has for you if your needs aren't met? How can you share His Word or teach others if you don't have food, clothes, or shelter? Would God ask you to join His army and then not give you the supplies you need? Of course not!

Read: PSALM 37:5

Your heart is like a greenhouse ready to grow good fruit. And your mind is the doorway to that greenhouse. It is in your mind that you decide which seeds are planted in your heart and which seeds are thrown away. Which thoughts are worth hanging on to and which ones need to be weeded out.

The Holy Spirit is ready to help you sort out all those thoughts that try to get in. He can help you guard your heart. He stands with you in the doorway. If a thought that may not be so good approaches, do you open the door wider? Of course not. You "capture every thought and make it give up and obey Christ" (2 Corinthians 10:5). You don't leave the door unguarded. You stand ready to capture any thought not good enough to enter.

Read: ROMANS 8:6

Do you know who you are? Let me tell you:

You are the brother or sister of Christ (Romans 8:17).

You are eternal—you will never die—just like the angels (Luke 20:36).

You have a crown that will last forever (1 Corinthians 9:25).

You are His treasured possession (Exodus 19:5).

But more than any of those things—more important than any title—is the simple fact that you are God's own child.

"We really are His children," and *you* really are His child. And because you are His child, if something is important to you, it's important to God.

Read: 1 JOHN 3:1

October 3

There are many things you can do for yourself, like tie your shoes, pour milk, and ride a bike.

There are many things that you dream of doing, like making the baseball team or the perfect layup, or learning to play the clarinet. You may even have dreams of what you will be when you grow up—a veterinarian, an astronaut, a teacher, or even a preacher. With hard work and study, you can make many of these dreams come true.

But the greatest dream is one that you can't do by yourself—no matter how hard you try. It's God's dream for you.

"God has a way to *make people right with Him*" (Romans 3:21). God's dream for you is not to make you rich or famous or popular. God's greatest dream is to make you right with Him.

Read: 1 JOHN 4:10

March 29

Have you ever tried to follow your dad through the snow or across the sand? Have you tried to step only in the footprints that he's made? Not an easy task! You have to stretch your legs as far as they will go to reach his footprints! But by following them, you know which way to go. That's what following God is like. It's called *discipleship*.

As a Christian, the footprints of your parents, grandparents, or teachers show you the right way to go, what to say and do as a child of God. No one has to walk this path alone.

Did you know that you also leave footprints? Even though you are young, you can lead others to Jesus. Part of discipleship is not letting someone walk this trail alone.

Read: JOHN 13:35

October 2

When we're living our lives for God, it's like He has put us in His navy and placed us on His ship. This ship has one purpose—to carry us safely to heaven.

But this is no cruise ship. It's a battleship. Each of us has a different job to do. Some are snatching sin-soaked people out of the water and pulling them onto God's boat of grace. Others are busy with the enemy, working the cannons of prayer and worship. Still others are feeding and training the crew. Each of us can tell the story of our personal meeting with the Captain because we've all met Him. We've followed Him across the gangplank of grace and onto His boat. Though the battle is fierce, the boat is safe, for our captain is God. This ship will not sink.

Read: ROMANS 12:5

Stop for a minute and think about the cross. Picture the soldiers' hands that nailed Jesus' hands to the cross. But it wasn't really the soldiers' hands who held Jesus' hands there. It was God and His love for each of us that held those hands on the cross.

Those same hands scooped out the oceans and built up the mountains. Those same hands set the sunrise in place and created each cloud. Those same hands designed an incredible plan to save you and me. Those hands could have reached out and called ten thousand angels to save Jesus from the cross.

But He didn't.

Why? Because those hands that made you and placed you on this planet also wrote this promise: "God would give up His only Son to save you." And so He did.

Read: PHILIPPIANS 2:8

October 1

Here is a scene that happens in Brazil thousands of times each day:

It's early morning. Time for young Marcos to leave for school. As he gathers his books and heads for the door, he stops by his father's chair. He looks into his father's face. "*Bênção, Pai*?" (Blessing, Father?) Marcos asks.

The father raises his hand. "*Deus te abençoe, meu filho*" (God bless you, my son), he says.

Then Marcos heads to school, knowing he has asked for a blessing and been given one with love by his father.

We should ask the same question of our heavenly Father—*Blessing, Father*? For just like the little child wanting his father's blessing, each of us needs a daily reminder of our heavenly Father's love.

Read: EPHESIANS 3:16

March 31

A day is coming when everyone will hear Jesus' voice. It's the day that Jesus returns from heaven. On that day all other voices will be silent. His voice—and only His voice—will be heard.

Some people will hear His voice for the very first time. It's not that He never spoke to them. It's just that they never listened. They will hear Him that one time—and then they will never hear Him again. They will spend eternity without Jesus.

But other people will hear Jesus' voice and will know who it is. They've been listening to Him and following Him because they are like the sheep who know the voice of their shepherd. Jesus will call His sheep by their names (John 10:3), and they will follow Him. And this time, they will follow Him into heaven.

Read: JOHN 5:28-29

My daughter Jenna and I once visited the city of Jerusalem. One afternoon we found ourselves behind an orthodox Jewish father and his three daughters. One of the girls, perhaps five years old, fell a few steps behind and couldn't see her father. "Abba!" she called to him. Her *abba*—her father—spotted her and immediately held out his hand.

When the light changed, he led her across the street. In the middle of the street, he reached down and swung her up into his arms, and they went on with their journey.

Isn't that what we all need? An *abba* who hears us when we call? Who takes our hand and guides us through the streets of life? Don't we all need an *abba* who swings us into his arms and carries us home? We all need a Father.

Read: PSALM 25:6

April 1

The cross didn't just happen. Jesus' death was not an accident. The cross wasn't a sad surprise. Calvary was not some cosmic mix-up or galactic goof. It wasn't some failed attempt to save the world. Jesus' death was anything but unexpected.

No, Jesus' death was part of God's incredible plan to save you, to save me, and to save all of His children. And that plan started thousands of years before Jesus came to earth.

The moment that forbidden fruit touched the lips of Eve, God had a plan to save us all. Although the cross wouldn't appear for centuries, the plan for it began in the garden of Eden. And between that moment in the garden and the moment the first nail went into the cross, God's great plan to save us was fulfilled.

Read: ACTS 2:23

September 29

The joy that filled the hearts of the very first Christians was their unshakable belief that Jesus truly was the Son of God. They believed that if Jesus had been only a man, He would have stayed in the tomb. These early Christians just couldn't stay silent about the fact that the One they saw die on a cross walked again on the earth and was seen by five hundred people.

Let us ask our Father God humbly, yet boldly in the name of Jesus, to help us remember the empty tomb. Let us see the victorious Jesus: the One who defeated the tomb and defeated death. And let us also remember that we, too, will one day be given that same victory. One day, we will defeat the tomb and defeat death.

Read: 1 CORINTHIANS 15:55

April 2

Some things are easy to do. But some things—like getting a shot, trying out for the team, or getting a tooth pulled—just aren't. There are times when we just have to *do* what we know we need to.

When Jesus went back to Jerusalem for the last time, He knew it wasn't going to be easy. It was by far the hardest thing any person has ever had to do. But He was determined to follow His Father's plan. And He knew He would have to die to do it (Luke 9:51).

Some people call it grace, salvation, or sacrifice. Jesus called it love. "For God loved the world so much that He gave His only Son. God gave His Son so that whoever believes in Him may not be lost, but have eternal life" (John 3:16).

Read: JOHN 1:29

September 28

God wants you to "think and act like Christ Jesus" (Philippians 2:5). But how? The answer is surprisingly simple. It takes just one decision: *I will let Jesus rule my thoughts.*

Jesus is the Ruler of heaven and earth. He has the final say on everything. Your classmates, for example, may say you're not cool enough to hang out with them. But Jesus says you are cool enough to inherit His kingdom.

Or suppose you want to cheat on a test. But Jesus has said that stealing is wrong, and that includes stealing answers. If you've decided to let Him rule over your ideas, then the idea of cheating cannot stay in your thoughts.

To have a pure heart, we must allow Jesus to rule over our thoughts. If we're willing to do that, He'll change us to be like Him.

Read: PROVERBS 4:23

April 3

In the Garden of Gethsemane, Jesus prayed about many things. But did you know that He also prayed about you? Jesus loved you so much that—in His last hours on earth—He just had to talk to God about you. He prayed that you would be with Him and that you would see His glory (John 17:24). And He prayed that God would keep you safe from the evils of this world (John 17:11).

And today, more than two thousand years later, God is still answering Jesus' prayer. He knows your troubles, your tough decisions, and even your temptations. He knows your every struggle to do the right thing, your every sadness, and your every joy. And He promises that He will always be right there with you to help you through (Matthew 28:20).

Read: LUKE 22:41

September 27

It's easy to thank God when He does what we want. But God doesn't always do what we want. Ask Job.

He lost everything, including his children and his health. Where did this misery come from? And where would help come from?

Job went straight to God and told Him his troubles. His head hurt. His body hurt. His heart hurt.

And God answered. Not with answers, but with questions. A whole ocean of questions!

After dozens of questions, Job got the point. What is it?

The point is this: God doesn't owe anyone anything. No reasons. No explanations. Nothing. If He gave them, we wouldn't be able to understand them anyway.

God is God. He knows what He is doing. And even when you don't understand, trust His heart and His love for you.

Read: JOB 42:3

Jesus told us to pray for the forgiveness of our sins and to forgive those who do wrong to us. When He said that, He knew that He would be the One to pay for those sins. He knew that He would hang on the cross. And He knew that He would say, "It is finished"... the debt for your sins is paid (John 19:30).

There are some facts that will never change. One fact is that you are forgiven. If you believe in Christ and follow Him, your sins are covered. When He sees you, He doesn't even see your sins. He sees you as better than you see yourself. And that is a wonderful fact of your life.

Read: ISAIAH 1:18

September 26

In the Sermon on the Mount, what Jesus promised is God's radical remake of our hearts.

Check out how it begins: First, we see that we are in need (we're poor in spirit). Next, we repent of trying to save ourselves (we mourn). We stop trying to be boss of our lives and give control to God (we're meek). We are so grateful for God's presence that we want more of Him (we hunger and thirst). As we grow closer to God, we become more like Him. We forgive others (we're merciful). We change our way of looking at things (we're pure in heart). We love others (we're peacemakers). We suffer through unfairness (we're persecuted).

This is no small change. It's tearing down the old self and creating the new. The greater the change, the greater the joy.

Read: MATTHEW 5:12

Worship. In two thousand years we still haven't figured it out. We still struggle with how to pray. We don't know when to kneel or stand. Worship can be confusing.

But God gave us Psalms to help us worship Him. And although the psalms talk about many different things, they each have the same purpose: to draw us closer to the heart of God.

Some psalms are bold. Others are humble. Some are to be sung. Others are to be prayed. Some seem written just for you alone. Others seem to be for the whole world to sing.

The fact that there are so many different kinds of psalms reminds us that there are many different kinds of worship. There is no one right way. Each person worships differently. But each person should worship.

Read: PSALM 95:6

September 25

It makes sense. Dads like giving their children special names. Princess. Tiger. Sweetheart. Bubba. Angel. So it makes sense that your heavenly Father would have a name for you.

And isn't it incredible to think that God has saved a name just for you? One you don't even know? We've always thought that the name we got when we were born is the name we will keep. Not so. The road ahead is so bright that a fresh, new name is needed. Your eternity is so special that no ordinary name will do.

God has one picked out just for you. There is more to your life than you ever thought. There is more to your story than what you have read.

And so I beg you...be there when God whispers your name.

Read: REVELATION 2:17

What Jesus dreamed of doing (saving us all) and what He had to do (face the cross) seemed impossible to Him. So Jesus prayed for the impossible to happen—that the cross would not be necessary.

The lesson here for us is that Jesus prayed. When it seemed that the world had turned against Him, when He felt all alone, when it seemed impossible for Him to do what He needed to do... Jesus prayed.

There may be times when it feels like everyone is against you. Maybe your friends are talking about you behind your back. Pray. There may be times when you feel all alone and that no one understands. Pray. There may even be times when it seems impossible for you to do what you know you need to do. Pray... just as Jesus did.

Read: JOHN 17:13

September 24

Being apart from the ones we love is hard. When death is the reason for our good-bye, it is especially tough. It is right for us to be sad and to cry, but we don't have to give up hope. Remember: They had pain here on earth, but they have no pain there in heaven. They struggled here on earth, but they have no struggles there in heaven.

You and I might wonder why God took them to heaven. But they don't. They understand. They are, at this very second, at peace and with God.

When it is cold here on earth, we can take comfort in knowing that our loved ones are safe in the warm arms of God. And when Jesus comes back, we will see them again.

Read: JOHN 11:25

The night that Jesus was arrested, there were many people gathered. Judas with his kiss of betrayal. Peter with his sword. The soldiers with their weapons. And though these are important, they aren't the most important. The true battle is not between Jesus and the soldiers; it is between God and Satan. But Satan doesn't have a chance.

Jesus speaks just three simple words—"I am Jesus"—and sends both the devil and members of the world's finest army falling to the ground (John 18:5–6). Neither Satan nor those who do his will can stand before Christ.

When Jesus says He will keep you safe, He means it. The devil will have to get through Him to get to you. Jesus protects you. When He says He will get you home to heaven, He will get you home.

Read: JOHN 10:19

September 23

Our human minds are not able to handle the thoughts of eternity in heaven. We can never understand a world without time or a place without a beginning or end. Our minds simply don't have the hooks on which to hang those kinds of thinking caps. So God becomes like the parent who says, "Just trust Me."

Don't be worried about things you can't understand. Many people look for clues and hidden messages, trying to figure out exactly when Christ will come back and exactly what that day will look like. But for the Christian, the return of Christ is not a riddle to be solved or a code to be broken. It is a day to be hoped for and waited for with joy and excitement. And until that day comes, we will trust God with our future.

Read: JOHN 14:1

When you look in the mirror, what do you see? Do you see your mistakes? Do you see the guy who lied to his mom about the broken picture? Do you see the girl who didn't stand up for a friend when she was being made fun of?

When your eyes look in the mirror, do you see a promise breaker? A bad friend? Someone who has messed up... again... and again... and again? If you do, then please look once more. But this time look through the eyes of faith. See what God sees. He sees His much-loved child, the one He sent His Son to save. Your eyes see your mistakes. But God's eyes see the child He loves.

Your eyes see your sin and guilt. But God's eyes see someone washed clean by the sacrifice of Jesus.

Read: EPHESIANS 6:10

September 22

Peter *feared* death and ran away. Gideon *feared* defeat and hid. Moses *feared* failure and begged God to choose someone else.

But faith begins when you are in the valley of *fear* and you look up to see *God* on the mountaintop. You see what you need—God. You see what you have—your fears and limited abilities. You know that you can't save yourself.

Moses had the sea in front of him and an army of Egyptian enemies behind. The Israelites could swim or fight, but neither choice was enough to save them.

Paul was a master of the Jewish laws. But one glimpse of Jesus on the road to Damascus proved that how much he knew would never be enough.

Faith that begins with fear brings you closer to the Father. You just need to look up.

Read: JOHN 14:8

It wasn't right for Judas to betray his friend Jesus.

It wasn't right that the ones Jesus came to save were the ones who hit Him, lied about Him, and spat upon Him.

And it wasn't right for the One who had never sinned to be punished for all of our sins.

It wasn't right, but it happened.

Why? It happened so that "he who believes in God's Son [would not be] judged guilty" (John 3:18).

Was it right? No. Was it fair? No. Was it love? Yes. Did it save you? Yes.

Read: EPHESIANS 3:19

September 21

You wouldn't open the door to a stranger, would you? You know how dangerous that can be. But let any trashy thought knock on the door of our mind, and we let it right in! Anger shows up, pity wants to have a party, jealousy rings the doorbell, and we say, "Welcome! Let me show you to the guest room." Don't we know how to say no?

For most of us, watching our thoughts is, well, *unthought* of. We watch our time, our clothes, our homework, even our hair. But not our thoughts. Shouldn't we be as worried about our thoughts as we are about everything else? Jesus was. Like a trained soldier at the gate of a city, He stood watch over His mind. He guarded the gate to His heart.

If Jesus did, shouldn't we?

Read: 1 PETER 5:8-9

All different kinds of people came to Jesus for help. In fact, it seems that everywhere Jesus went, great crowds of people came to Him, wanting His help.

There must have been times when He was tired and wanted to rest. Why didn't He turn them away? Why didn't He take a day off now and then? Why?

Could it be that Jesus' heart hurt for those people? Could it be that His heart was—and is—broken for all people who have ever cried out in prayer, "Why is this happening to me?"

Imagine Jesus today, bending down close to someone who is hurt. He's listening. His eyes fill with tears as He hears that person's troubles. Then His hand gently brushes away a tear. He was hurt once too. He understands.

Read: MATTHEW 9:36

September 20

Some years ago a sociologist—a person who studies how people act—went with some mountain climbers on an expedition. He noticed there was a connection between clouds and contentment. Where there were no clouds and the climbers could see the peak of the mountain, they were full of energy and eager to help one another. But when dark, gray clouds blocked their view of the mountaintop, the climbers became bad-tempered and selfish.

The same thing happens to us. As long as our eyes are on God's majesty, we are happy with ourselves and happy to help others. But let our eyes focus on the dirt of this world, and we will grumble about every rock and mud puddle. Paul urged us to "think only about the things in heaven, not the things on earth" (Colossians 3:2).

Read: 1 PETER 1:8

April 11

It was the day of Jesus' crucifixion. God looked around and saw the scene. Three men hung on three crosses. Arms spread. Heads fallen forward. They moaned with the wind.

Some Roman soldiers sat on the ground near the three crosses. Heartbroken women huddled at the foot of the hill...their faces streaked with tears.

The Bible tells us that all heaven stood ready to fight—"12 armies of angels" could have been sent to save Jesus (Matthew 26:53). All nature rose up, ready to rescue Him as darkness covered the "whole country" and "the earth shook and rocks broke apart" (Matthew 27:45, 51). Still the angels waited to protect. But the Creator never gave the order to save His Son.

Imagine the scene in heaven: "It must be done," God said, as He turned away. The angel whispered, "It would be less painful if..." But the Creator interrupted softly, "But it wouldn't be love."

Read: JOHN 3:16

September 19

The writer of Hebrews takes us on a Discovery Channel–style tour of heaven. Listen to how he describes the mountaintop of Zion. He says when we reach the mountain we will have come to "the city of the living God, the heavenly Jerusalem. You have come to thousands of angels gathered with joy. You have come to the meeting of God's firstborn children. Their names are written in heaven. You have come to God" (Hebrews 12:22–23).

What a mountain! Won't it be great to meet the angels? Imagine the meeting! A gathering of all God's children. No jealousy. No popular and unpopular. No in-crowd and out-crowd. We will all be perfect... sinless.

And imagine seeing God. Face-to-face. To finally gaze into your Father's eyes. To see Him looking at you. For all eternity.

Read: PSALM 134:3

Pretend you are at the foot of the cross. Listen for a moment. Imagine the sound of Jesus' cry from the cross. The sky is dark. The other two men are moaning on their crosses. The loud jeers of the crowd are finally silent. Perhaps there is thunder, or crying, or silence. Then Jesus draws a deep breath, pushes His feet downward on that Roman nail, and cries, "It is finished!"

What was finished? God's plan for saving all of mankind. The plan that had started in the garden of Eden was done at last. God had given His greatest gift to each of us. He had washed away our every sin and will one day take us home to heaven. And with that gift came God's message of how much He loves each and every one of us.

Read: JOHN 19:30

September 18

Hatred can sneak up on you. It usually starts with something tiny, like a scratch on your new bike. Then it builds. Every time you climb on your bike, that scratch is all you see. You didn't see who did it, but you bet you can describe him. Big kid, wart on his chin, bully, kicks kittens for fun.

Let me be clear. Hatred will sour your attitude and break your back. The load of anger is simply too heavy to carry. Your knees will buckle and your heart will break beneath the weight. The mountain of life is steep and hard enough to climb without a load of hatred on your back. The only good choice is for you to drop the anger.

God will never ask you to give anyone more grace than He's already given you.

Read: EPHESIANS 4:31

God's promise to those who choose to follow Jesus is simple: because Jesus was raised from the dead—*resurrected*—we, too, will rise from death and go to live in heaven with Him.

But can we trust that promise? How do we know the resurrection was real? That isn't just a good question. It is *the* best question. Paul wrote, "If Christ has not been raised, then your faith is for nothing; you are still guilty of your sins" (1 Corinthians 15:17).

In other words, if Christ has been raised from the dead, then His followers will join Him in heaven. But if He has not been raised, then His followers are lost forever.

Aren't you glad the tomb really was *empty*?

Read: 1 THESSALONIANS 4:14

September 17

God has many names to show how He meets your many needs.

When you're confused about the future, go to your *Jehovah-raah*, your caring Shepherd. When you're worried about the things you need, talk to *Jehovah-jireh*, the Lord who Provides. Do your troubles seem too large? Seek the help of *Jehovah-shalom*, the Lord is Peace. Are you sick or hurting? *Jehovah-rophe*, the Lord who Heals, will see you now. Do you feel like a soldier stuck behind enemy lines? Keep your eyes on *Jehovah-nissi*, the Lord is the Flag that I follow.

Thinking about the names of God reminds you of the character of God. Take these names and hide them in your heart.

God is...the Shepherd who guides, the *Lord* who provides, the Voice who brings peace, the *Physician* who heals, and the *Flag* that the soldier follows.

Read: PROVERBS 18:10

Mary and Mary Magdalene made their way up the mountain toward Jesus' tomb. They were taking spices to put on His body. It was something that needed to be done. They didn't expect anything in return. After all, what could Jesus give them? What could a dead man offer them? These two women weren't going to Jesus' tomb to *get* anything; they were going to *give*. They were going because they wanted to serve Him... because they loved Him.

There is no greater reason.

At the tomb that day, Mary and Mary Magdalene were acting out of love—the greatest service of all. It is what we are called to do as Jesus' disciples. It is truly following Him.

Read: MATTHEW 28:1

September 16

Think for a moment about who God really is and what He does for us:

He doesn't say it's okay to sin, and He doesn't change His definition of holiness.

He doesn't ignore our disobedience, and He expects us to try to be better every day.

When we sin, those sins must be punished. But—incredibly—God chooses to wipe those sins away from us and place them on His Son instead. Jesus takes the punishment for our sins.

So our sins are punished, but we are not. We are forgiven!

God does what we cannot do, so that we can be what we wouldn't even dare to dream of: *perfect before God*.

Read: PSALM 89:8

Mary and Mary Magdalene knew Jesus' body needed to be covered with special spices before He could be buried. That's what the Jews did for people who had died. No one else volunteered, so the Marys decided to do it (Mark 16:1–2).

What would have happened if, on the way to the tomb, they had changed their minds? What if they had given up? What if one had thrown up her hands and moaned, "I'm tired of being the only one who cares. Let Andrew do something for a change. Let Nathanael take a turn"?

That would have been so sad. You see, we know something they didn't. We know the Father was watching. Mary and Mary thought they were alone. They weren't. God knew—just as He knows all the good that you do.

Read: COLOSSIANS 3:17

September 15

Are you in a sticky situation, wondering if you should tell the truth or not? The question to ask at times like these is, "Will God bless my lies?" Will He bless a plan built on fibs and falsehoods? Will the Lord—who loves the truth—bless this web of lies? Will God honor the schoolwork of a cheat?

No, I don't think so either.

Take a look inside your heart. Ask some tough questions: *Am I being totally honest with my mom and dad*? *Are my words truthful*? *What about at school*? *Am I honest with my teachers*? *Am I a trustworthy student*? *An honest friend*?

Do you tell the truth...always? If not, start today. Don't wait until tomorrow to be truthful. The ripple of today's lies will become tomorrow's wave of fibs and next year's flood of falsehood.

Read: EPHESIANS 4:25

April 16

Tolerance is a big word that you hear a lot these days. The world thinks it means accepting other people's beliefs about religion. But for Jesus, tolerance meant being kind to those who didn't understand His truth. And it meant helping them to understand. For example, He was tolerant of the disciples when they doubted; of the crowds when they misunderstood; of us when we sin.

But there is one thing about which Jesus was not—and is not—tolerant. He is not tolerant about other ideas of how to get to heaven.

Some people believe if they do enough good things, or if they are strong enough, they'll get to heaven. Others believe there are many different ways to heaven. But the truth is that there is only one way to heaven—by believing in and obeying Jesus.

Read: JOHN 14:6

September 14

What if someone made a movie about your hands? What would we see?

Everyone's movie would start much the same, with an infant's fist, then a close-up of a tiny hand wrapped around Mom's finger.

If you showed the movie to your friends, you'd be proud of some moments: your hands holding out a gift, patting a friend on the back, helping up someone who's fallen, taking food to the sick. But then there are other scenes. Hands taking instead of giving, snatching instead of offering, hitting instead of helping.

Oh, the power of our hands! Leave them uncontrolled, and they become weapons: clawing, scratching, and snatching for our own selfish wants. But control them and our hands become tools of grace and kindness—not just tools in the hands of God, but God's very own hands.

Read: JOB 17:9

Pretend you have a bank account in heaven—a "holiness account."

In order to get into heaven, your account must be full. So you try to fill it by doing as many good things as you can. You say something nice to a friend, help your neighbor rake leaves, or help in the church nursery. You lead prayers or memorize Bible verses. Doing more good things should fill up your holiness account, right?

Wrong. You can never earn enough holiness. To get to heaven, God demands that your holiness account be full— and you just can't do that on your own. So how *do* you get to heaven? Jesus.

When you choose to believe in Jesus and to obey Him, He fills up your holiness account for you. It's called *grace*—and it's His gift to you.

Read: ROMANS 4:5

September 13

When I was ten years old, my mother made me take piano lessons. Spending thirty minutes every afternoon on that piano bench was torture.

Some of the music, though, I learned to enjoy. I hammered the staccatos. I pounded the crescendos. But there was one instruction in the music I could never get quite right. The *rest*. That zigzag-looking sign to do nothing. What sense does that make? Why sit at the piano and pause when you can pound?

"Because," my teacher patiently explained, "music is always sweeter after a rest."

It didn't make sense to me then. But now my teacher's words ring with wisdom—divine wisdom. Music is sweeter after a rest. And life is sweeter after you rest in the Lord.

Read: EXODUS 20:11

April 18

Many people believe that it was the iron nails that held Jesus on the cross. But it wasn't. Not really. Love held Jesus on the cross.

Jesus knew that our sins had to be punished, and He loved us so much that He took our punishment for us. Jesus—who had never sinned—took on all of our sins and let them die on the cross with Him.

God could have sent His army of angels to save Jesus, but He didn't—because God would rather give up His Son than give up on getting us to heaven.

No matter what you've done or said, it's never too late to talk to God about it, ask for forgiveness, and be free from all sin and guilt.

What makes you a Christian is not that you're perfect but that you're *forgiven*.

Read: 2 CORINTHIANS 5:21

September 12

This world is all about living. Death is seen as the end of everything. But God takes a very different view of life and death. For God, death is not the end—it is the beginning. What we see as the greatest sadness, He sees as the greatest victory.

A seed must die and be buried before it can grow. So when a Christian dies, it's not just a time for sadness; it is a time to trust. Like the seed, the body is buried. And just as a buried seed sprouts new life, so our body will blossom into a new body.

The seeds of the Christians' bodies buried in the earth will blossom in heaven. Our souls and bodies will be one again, and we will be like Jesus.

Read: JOHN 12:24

April 19

The white space between the lines of the Bible verses leaves room for lots of questions. You can hardly read Scripture without whispering, "I wonder..."

"I wonder if Eve ever ate any more fruit."

"I wonder if Noah had trouble sleeping during thunderstorms."

"I wonder if Jonah ever wanted to eat fish for dinner."

But in your wonderings, there are some questions you never need to ask: Does God care? Do you matter to God? Does He still love His children?

God sent a tiny baby to be born in a stable. That was the proof that, yes, God cares.

Yes, your sins are forgiven. Yes, your name is written in heaven. And, yes, God is in your world.

Immanuel means "God is with us"... and He is.

Read: MATTHEW 1:23

September 11

Do-it-yourself is something you hear a lot these days. You can learn to build your own clubhouse, decorate your own room, bake your own birthday cake. There are a lot of things that you can do yourself. But there is no such thing as a do-it-yourself way to heaven.

To get to heaven, we need help. *Real help*. Not just happy words and a pat on the back. We need real help from the One who really loves us. Real help from the One with real power.

We need help from the One who knows our thoughts before we think them and our feelings before we feel them. We need help from the inside out. And the great news is that the Spirit of God will come to live inside us when we choose to follow Him.

Read: JOHN 14:16-17

Want to know God's will for your life? Then answer this question: What do you feel that you just *have to do* to show God's love or to help others?

Pay attention to your heart! Do you love to sing? Then sing! Does your heart hurt for the sick and the lonely? Then comfort them!

As a young man, I felt God wanted me to preach. But I wasn't sure if I understood God's will correctly. So I talked to a minister whom I looked up to. His advice to me was, "Don't preach unless you *have* to."

As I thought about his words, I found my answer. "I have to preach. If I don't, I'll spend the rest of my life wishing that I had."

What is it that you just *have to do* for God?

Read: PSALM 40:8

September 10

We want more than this earth can give us. We wish for a place free of pain and hunger, sickness, tears, loss. Sometimes we find ourselves asking, "Why is life so hard?"

So God gives us moments of joy. The loving hug of a parent, the comfort of a friend, the warm sunshine. These are His gifts of hope to us—like tiny slivers of light from heaven. God gives us these glimpses to keep us going. He's saying to us, "If you think this is good, just wait and see what I have for you in heaven."

"No one has ever imagined what God has prepared for those who love Him" (1 Corinthians 2:9). Amazing! Heaven is *beyond* our imagination. Even in our most creative moments, in our wildest dreams, we cannot imagine the wonder and perfection of heaven.

Read: ECCLESIASTES 3:10

How long has it been since you let God have your full attention? I mean *really* have it. How long since you've gone without any computers or television or telephones? How long since you just listened for His voice and did nothing else? That's what Jesus did. He set aside time to spend time with just God.

If you read about Jesus in the Bible, you'll see that He made time with God a habit. He spent time with God regularly, praying and listening. Mark said, "Early the next morning, Jesus woke and left the house while it was still dark. He went to a place to be alone and pray" (Mark 1:35).

If Jesus—the Son of God, the Savior who never sinned— thought He needed to take time to pray, wouldn't we be smart to do the same?

Read: LUKE 5:16

September 9

Acts of faith aren't usually born out of peace and calm. It wasn't military know-how that made Moses raise his staff on the bank of the Red Sea. He was between an army and an ocean.

It wasn't medical research that convinced Naaman to dip seven times in the river. He was a very sick man. It wasn't common sense that caused Paul to abandon the Jewish laws he'd followed his whole life and follow Jesus. He couldn't see any other way.

And it wasn't a bold bunch who prayed in Jerusalem for Peter's release from prison. It was a frightened, desperate band of backed-into-a-corner believers with no other choice. A bunch of have-nots begging for help. And they were never stronger.

For at the beginning of every act of faith, there is often a seed of fear.

Read: ACTS 16:25

April 22

When you get to heaven, something wonderful will happen. One final change will happen. You will be just like Jesus.

Of all the blessings in heaven, one of the greatest will be you! You will be God's *magnum opus*. That means that you will be His masterpiece, His *greatest* work of art. The angels will gasp in amazement. God's work in you will be complete. As last you will have a heart just like His.

You will love with a perfect love.

You will worship with a joyful face.

You'll hear each word God speaks.

Your heart and your thoughts will be pure; your words will be like jewels—beautiful gifts to those who hear them.

You will be just like Jesus. Finally, you will have a heart like His.

Read: 1 JOHN 3:2

September 8

There are only so many hours in the day. Who gets them? You know what I'm talking about, don't you? "The student council needs a new treasurer. You're not afraid to speak in groups, you're good at organization, and you've got an A+ in math. You're perfect for the job!"

It's a tug-of-war, and you are the rope. Family, church, homework, chores, sports, hobbies, friends—how do you choose what gets your time? Ask the One who created time how He wants you to spend it. His answer might be:

Blessed are those who see the jobs God wants them to do.

Blessed are those who know that there is only one God, that He is in charge.

Blessed are those who ask Him *what on earth* they are on earth to do—and they do it.

Read: 1 PETER 4:10

April 23

Because of Jesus' sacrifice on the cross, our past sins are forgiven and our future in heaven is certain. "We have been made right with God because of our faith. So we have peace with God through our Lord Jesus Christ" (Romans 5:1).

What is *peace with God* like? Have you even been in a gym filled with people cheering for their team? Or at a concert with loud music? Or stuck between two people screaming at each other? And then...you stepped outside. Your heart stopped pounding, your breathing slowed. How quiet, how... peaceful.

When you get to heaven, there will be no more screaming, loudness, or arguing. There will be only love and joy and peace. Better than peace between countries, peace between friends, and peace at home—We will have peace with God.

Read: JOHN 15:15

God has a strict rule about honesty.

From Genesis to Revelation, that rule is the same: God loves the truth and hates lies. In 1 Corinthians 6:9–10, Paul listed the types of people who will not be in the kingdom of heaven. The group he described is a ragged mixture of those who worship idols, get drunk, rob people, and—there it is—*lie about others*.

Such a strict rule may surprise you. *You mean my fibbing and little white lies make God as angry as drugs and drunkenness*? Yes.

Why the hard line? Why the tough stand?

For one reason: God is truth, so lying is the exact opposite of the nature of God.

Read: PROVERBS 12:22

If we're already forgiven for our sins, then why does Jesus teach us to pray, "Forgive the sins we have done" (Matthew 6:12)?

For the very same reason your parents and teachers ask you to apologize. If my own children break a rule, I don't kick them out of the house or tell them to change their last name. But I do want them to be honest about what they did. And until they do, our relationship will suffer. I'll still be their dad, and they will still be my children, but we won't be as close. There will be a wall between us.

The same thing happens in your walk with God. You will always be His child, but confessing sins makes your relationship better. Confessing your sins gets you closer to God.

Read: PSALM 32:1

September 6

I've heard people talk about the story of Ananias and Sapphira (Acts 5:1–11) with a nervous chuckle and say, "I'm glad God doesn't still strike people dead for lying." But it seems to me that the punishment for lying is still death. Not death of the body, maybe, but death of: *a parent's trust*—lies are like termites in the trunk of the family tree; *a conscience*—it's always easier to tell the second lie than the first; *a future*—just ask the student who was flunked for cheating.

We could also list the deaths of friendships, trust, peace, reputation, and self-respect. But perhaps the most tragic death that happens because of our lies is the death of our Christian witness. Courtrooms and judges won't listen to witnesses who lie. And neither will the world.

Read: PSALM 101:7

God doesn't keep the way to heaven a secret. His Word tells us how to get there. But even those who have never heard of Jesus are given a message about God: "The heavens tell the glory of God" (Psalm 19:1).

Nature is God's first missionary. If a person has nothing but nature, then nature is enough to tell him something about God. "Day after day [the heavens] tell the story.... They have no speech or words. They don't make any sound to be heard. But their message goes out through all the world. It goes everywhere on earth" (Psalm 19:2-4).

The wonders of nature can cause those who don't know God to wonder about their Creator. And God promises that those who search for Him with all their hearts will find Him (Jeremiah 29:13).

Read: ROMANS 1:20

Have you had too many disappointments this week? One too many defeats lately and not nearly enough victories? Read the story of the disciples on the road to Emmaus in Luke 24:13–35. The Savior they thought was dead was now walking right beside them. He went into their house and sat at their table. And then something happened in their hearts: "When Jesus talked to us on the road, it felt like a fire burning in us. It was exciting when He explained the true meaning of the Scriptures" (Luke 24:32).

Next time you're disappointed, don't give up. Just be patient and let God remind you that He's still in control. Let Him warm your heart with His Word. After all, it ain't over till it's over.

Read: HEBREWS 10:23

A legend from India tells about a mouse who was terrified of cats until a magician agreed to change him into a cat. That fixed his fear... until he met a dog. So the magician changed him into a dog. The mouse-turned-cat-turned-dog was happy... until he met a tiger. On and on it went, until the magician would not help. "I will make you into a mouse again, for... you still have the heart of a mouse."

Lots of people look tough on the outside, but inside they are trembling with fear. We fight fear, and we try to make ourselves safe by wearing the right clothes, hanging out with the right friends, and having the right stuff. But does that really work?

Courage comes from who we are inside—God's children— not what we have on the outside.

Read: PSALM 31:24

September 4

Here is a big question: What is God doing when you are in trouble? When your lifeboat springs a leak and you're sinking fast? When the parachute doesn't open? When your tummy is empty and so are your pockets?

I know what we are doing. Nibbling on our nails like corn on the cob. Pacing the floors. Wringing our hands.

But what does God do?

He fights for us. He steps in front of us, protects us with His presence, and takes over. "You will only need to remain calm. The Lord will fight for you" (Exodus 14:14).

His job is to fight. Our job is to trust.

Just trust. Not take over. Or question. Our job is to pray and wait.

Read: PSALM 62:6

In my closet hangs a sweater that is too small. I should throw it away. But *love* won't let me.

My mom made it for me. Each stitch shows her love for me. Each strand was chosen with care. Each thread was picked with affection. It is special not because of what it is, but because of who made it.

That must have been what the writer of Psalm 139 was thinking when he wrote, "You knit me together in my mother's womb" (v. 13 NIV).

Think about those words. You were knit together by God. You were deliberately planned, specially gifted, and lovingly placed on this earth by Him. In a world that decides your worth by the clothes you wear or the sports you play, let me tell you something—you are valuable because God created you.

Read: PSALM 139:13

September 3

The most powerful life is the most simple life. It's the life that knows God is its source of strength. It's the life that stays free of clutter and busyness.

Being busy is not a sin. Jesus was busy. Paul was busy. Peter was busy. Nothing important happens without hard work and tiredness.

But what are we being busy about? Is it an endless chase to get more stuff? Or an endless search for popularity? That kind of busyness will leave you empty inside. That isn't pleasing to God.

Chasing after the things of this world just makes you tired. Stuff can't make you happy. Your stuff, your pride, your popularity—these are just things. When you try to make a life out of things instead of God, you only make yourself tired and unhappy.

Read: MATTHEW 6:21

Tell me, what did the thief on the cross do to deserve help? What right did he have to pray, "Jesus, remember me when you come into your kingdom!" (Luke 23:42)?

Well, he had the same right to ask Jesus to save him as we do.

Have we used every second of our time as we should? Have we ever laughed at someone or made fun of them? Do we deserve Jesus' help? Definitely not.

We could never do enough good to get us to heaven. In the single most important way of all, we are just like that thief—our only hope of getting into heaven is Jesus.

So, just like the thief, we pray, "Jesus, remember me."

And just like the thief, we hear the voice of Jesus say, "You will be with me in paradise!"

Read: LUKE 23:43

September 2

The freedom Jesus offers doesn't come through having more rights, but giving up yours. It's not about controlling everything, but giving up your control to Him. And it's not about collecting the stuff of this world, but giving it away.

Sounds strange, doesn't it? God wants to *free* His people by having them surrender to Him. God wants us to be His sons and daughters, not slaves to the stuff of this world. He wants us to be ruled by His love.

By believing that Jesus died for our salvation, we are freed from trying to work our way to heaven. We are free to pray and to love God with all our hearts. And we are free from our sins because we have been forgiven by the only One who can call us guilty. We are truly free!

Read: EPHESIANS 1:7

Some of us have tried to have a quiet time with God every day, but we have not stuck with it. Others of us have a hard time being still and quiet. Rather than spend time with God, listening for His voice, we let others do it and then tell us what God said. After all, isn't that what preachers and parents are for?

If your ideas about God come only from others and not from spending time with Him yourself, think about this: Do you do that with other parts of your life?

Do you let other people go on vacation for you, play with your friends for you, or eat for you? No, there are some things that no one else can do for you. Only you can.

And one of those things is spending time with God.

Read: JAMES 4:8

September 1

We are thirsty.

Not for fame, stuff, or popularity. Oh, we think that's what we want. Maybe we've tried those things. Maybe we've tasted those waters. But they won't quench our thirst—they just make us thirstier. Why? Because we aren't thirsty for the things of this world. We are thirsty for God and His goodness.

Matthew 5:6 says, "Those who want to do right more than anything else are happy."

Those who want to do right—that's righteousness. That's it. That's what we are actually thirsty for. We're thirsty for a clean heart. We crave a "do over." When we mess up, we want a fresh start. So we pray that God will reach down and do for us the one thing we can't do for ourselves—make us right again. And when we ask Him to, He promises that He will.

Read: PSALM 51:10

Jesus teaches us to pray, "Forgive the sins we have done... [and] do not cause us to be tested" (Matthew 6:12–13).

We've all made mistakes, and we'll all make some more. Paul asked, "So why do you judge your brother in Christ? And why do you think that you are better than he is? We will all stand before God, and he will judge us all" (Romans 14:10).

Do you have a brother or sister who could use some grace from you? It's better to forgive rather than to try to get even. Sometimes tattling and getting revenge only make things worse. And as for your brother, there comes a time when the best thing you can do is love him. Offer him the same grace and forgiveness that you've been given.

Read: MATTHEW 6:11-12

August 31

For all its strange names and unusual events, the Bible has a simple story: God made people. People turned away from God. God won't give up until He wins His people back. God will whisper. He will shout. He will touch and tug. He will take away our worries and fears. He will even take away our blessings. If there are 1,000 steps between us and Him, He will take 999. But He will leave the last step for us to take. The choice is ours.

Please understand. God's goal is not to make you happy. His goal is to make you His. His goal is not to get you what you want. It is to get you what you need—a faith in His Son that will get you to heaven.

Read: HOSEA 2:19

May 1

You and I live in a loud world. It's not easy to get someone's attention. That person must be willing to turn down the radio, turn away from the computer, turn the corner of the page, and put down the book. When someone in our world is willing to turn off everything else to listen to us, it is a gift. But in heaven God is always listening. Your prayers are like precious jewels to Him.

Your prayers on earth stir up God's power in heaven, and "what [God wants] will be done, here on earth as it is in heaven" (Matthew 6:10).

Your prayers move God to change the world. You may not understand the power and the mystery of prayer. You don't need to. But this much is clear: God is always listening, and He is always answering.

Read: 1 PETER 3:12

August 30

Have you ever seen a courtroom scene where a witness is telling the court what he knows? We are called to testify just like witnesses in a courtroom. We are to tell others what we've seen and heard about Jesus. Our job is not to make things seem different from what they are. Our job is to tell the truth. Period.

There is, however, one difference. Sooner or later, the witness in court will finish and step down from the witness chair. But as a witness for Christ, you never step down.

Because the promises of Jesus are always on trial, you must always be a witness. You must always tell the world who He is, what He has done for you, and what He wants to do for the world.

And you must always tell the truth.

Read: ACTS 1:8

When Peter asked to walk out on the water, he was not testing Jesus—he was begging. Stepping into a stormy sea did not make sense. But Peter grabbed the edge of the boat, threw out one leg, and then followed with the other leg. It was if an invisible pathway of rocks ran under his feet. At the end of the path was the glowing face of an "I'll-never-give-up-on-you" Friend—Jesus.

Like Peter, we try to do it all on our own. We only pray to Jesus when we realize that we need Him. When we realize we can't save ourselves, we call out to Him and beg Him to save us.

But when we do call out to Jesus, He answers us just as He answered Peter. He says, "Come" (Matthew 14:29).

Read: MATTHEW 14:28

August 29

What do we know about how our bodies will look in heaven? Will we look so different that others won't know who we are? Maybe. (We may need name tags.)

Will we be walking through walls and on water? Chances are we'll be doing much more than that.

Will we still have the scars from this life? The bumps, bruises, disease, jagged scars of bike wrecks, and broken arms. Will these still be on our bodies? That's a good question. Jesus kept the wounds on His hands, His feet, and His side for at least forty days. Will we keep ours? My opinion is no. Peter told us "we are healed because of His wounds" (1 Peter 2:24). In heaven, only one wound is worthy of being remembered—the wound of Jesus.

Our wounds and hurts will be healed.

Read: PHILIPPIANS 3:21

Can you imagine what would happen if your parents gave you everything you asked for on your next trip? You'd end up crawling with a bloated belly from one ice-cream store to the next.

And what if God gave us everything we asked for?

"God did not *choose* us to suffer His anger, but to have salvation through our Lord Jesus Christ" (1 Thessalonians 5:9).

What does God choose for your life? Salvation. God's greatest want is that you reach heaven. His plan includes stops that will help you. He frowns on stops that slow you down. When His perfect plan and your earthly plan crash together, a choice must be made. Who's in charge of this journey? You or God?

It's God. And I'm glad He chose heaven for us all.

Read: COLOSSIANS 4:2

We were made to live with God in heaven, but on earth we must live by trusting in God.

We must trust God, that He will do what is best and that He knows what is ahead. Look at Isaiah 57:1–2: "Good people are taken away, but no one understands. Those who do right are being taken away from evil and are given peace" (NCV).

Wow! What a thought. God takes good people away from the evil. Could death be part of God's grace? It isn't always easy to understand why good people get sick, or hurt, or even die. But we can always believe that God does what is best for each of His children. He's always taking care of us—especially in times of sickness and death.

Trust in God, Jesus encourages us, *and trust in Me*.

Read: PROVERBS 3:5

God gave us the Bible so that He could tell us His plan for us. The Bible tells us that we are all lost and need to be saved. And it tells us that Jesus is God in human form and that He was sent to save God's children.

The Bible was written by at least forty different authors spread out over sixteen hundred years. But it has just one message: salvation comes through faith in Jesus. One thread holds the whole Bible together: God's love for His children and God's plan to save them.

The Bible is like your compass for your journey through life. Check your compass, and you'll journey safely. Forget to use your compass—forget to study your Bible—and who knows where you'll end up.

Read: PSALM 119:105

Look at Paul's goal: *to bring each one into God's presence as a mature person in Christ*. Paul dreamed of the day that each person would be safe in Christ. What was his way of doing this? *Warning* and *teaching* others. What were Paul's tools? Verbs. Nouns. Sentences. Lessons. The same tools that you and I have. Was it easier back then to teach others than it is now? I don't think so. Paul called it work. "To do this, I work and struggle," he wrote. *Struggle* means it was hard. *Work* means homes visited, people taught, classes prepared.

How did Paul do it? What was his source of strength? It was Jesus—"Christ's great strength that works so powerfully in me."

As Paul worked, so did God. And as you work, so does the Father.

Read: COLOSSIANS 1:28-29

Every moment of your life, your accuser—Satan, the biggest tattletale of all time— is taking notes. He has noticed every mistake and written down every slip-up.

Satan has no greater goal than to take you to God's courtroom and press charges. He yells, "This one You call Your child, God, he doesn't deserve Your forgiveness. He's made too many mistakes."

As he speaks, you hang your head. You know he is right. "I plead guilty, Your Honor," you mumble.

"What is the sentence?" Satan asks.

"The punishment for sin is death," explains the Judge, "but Jesus Christ died as payment for this person's sins."

Satan suddenly has nothing to say. And you are filled with joy. You have stood before the Judge and heard Him say, "Not guilty!"

Read: ROMANS 8:33

August 26

The Bible calls Jesus the Shepherd and us His sheep. I wonder if Jesus doesn't give a slight grin as He sees one of His lost sheep come dragging into the fold—the broken, dirty sheep who stands at the door asking, "Can I come in?" The Shepherd looks down at the sheep and says, "Come in. This is your home."

Jesus has given you salvation. But *sanctification*—being made holy—will happen your whole life. Sanctification is being changed to be just a little bit more like Jesus each day. It is putting away the old sinfulness and taking on the new holiness.

The psalmist David told us that those who have been *redeemed*—who have been saved—will say so! If we're not saying so, maybe it's because we've forgotten what it's like to be saved.

Read: COLOSSIANS 3:10

Sometimes it may seem like Satan is winning the battle and that he is in charge. But God is in *complete* control, and He has a way of using Satan's evil plans to do good. Satan thought he'd won when Jesus died on the cross. But God raised Jesus from the dead and gave us the gift of salvation.

Many Christians in the early church were thrown in prison or killed. Many others left their homes and ran away to other lands. But God used those hard times to spread His word to other countries. Sad things and even bad things happen to all people—to those who believe in God and those who don't. But God has a special promise for His children: "In everything God works for the good of those who love Him" (Romans 8:28).

Read: 1 JOHN 4:4

When you realize that God has saved you, you'll want to praise Him like never before.

Maybe you haven't yet seen some of the tougher, stormier parts of life. If you haven't needed God to rescue you, you might have an easier time keeping Him at a distance. Sure He's important, but so are your grades. Your friends. Your sports and hobbies.

But maybe you *have* seen some of life's storms. The move, the divorce, the lost friend. Sadness might have fallen over you like a fog. In your heart, you weren't sure where to turn.

Turn to your friends for help? Only if you want to hide from the storm instead of escape it. Lean on your grades for strength? A storm isn't impressed with how much you know.

Only God can help you through all of life's storms.

Read: JOHN 5:24

Do you ever give in and decide to sin today, thinking, *Oh, I'll just confess tomorrow*?

It's easy to say, "I'm going to do whatever I want, because God will forgive me anyway."

But is that the purpose of grace? Of God's forgiveness? Did God give up His Son just so that we could get away with disobeying Him? Nope. The Bible tells us that "God's grace... teaches us not to live against God and not to do the evil things the world wants to do. That grace teaches us to live on earth now in a wise and right way" (Titus 2:11–12).

God's grace washes away all our selfish and sinful mistakes. Once we are clean, why would we want to go back to being dirty?

Read: TITUS 2:14

A lot of people will ask you, "What do you want to be when you grow up?" But a more important question is: "*Who* do you want to be?"

When it comes to what you want to be, there are hundreds of choices—from architect to zookeeper. But when it comes to *who* you want to be, there are only two choices: a person of the world or a person of God.

A person of the world thinks, *What do I want to do?* But a person of God thinks, *What does God want me to do?* See the difference?

A person of the world is always selfish and bragging. A person of God tries to obey Philippians 2:3: "Do not let selfishness or pride be your guide. Be humble and give more honor to others than to yourselves."

Read: GALATIANS 5:22–23

We laugh at the boy who stumbles this morning, but we didn't see how hard he was hit yesterday. We make fun of the girl with the limp, but we cannot see the rock in her shoe. Is someone too loud? Maybe he is afraid of being ignored again. Is someone else scared? Maybe she is afraid of failing again. We don't know. Only the One who is always watching them can know.

Not only do we not know about their yesterdays, but we don't know about their tomorrows. We must leave the judging to God. Our job is to "be kind and humble" to each other (1 Peter 3:8). Remember, "God began doing a good work in you. And He will continue it until it is finished when Jesus Christ comes again" (Philippians 1:6). God's not finished yet!

Read: MATTHEW 7:2

"With one sacrifice He made perfect forever those who are being made holy" (Hebrews 10:14).

Underline the word *perfect*. Note that the word is not *better*. Not *improving*. Not *looking brighter*. God doesn't just improve; He perfects. He doesn't make better; He completes.

Now I know that in one way we're not perfect. We still make mistakes. We still mess up. We still do exactly what we don't want to do, what we're trying so hard not to do. And that part of us is the part that God says is "being made holy."

But when it comes to our place before God, we're perfect. When He sees each of us, He sees one who has been made perfect through the One who is perfect—Jesus Christ.

Read: HEBREWS 10:17

If you have the right tools, you can learn to listen to God. What are those tools? Here are the ones I have found helpful:

The first is *a regular time and place*. Pick a time in your day and a corner of your world, and make that your time and place for God.

A second tool you need is *an open Bible*. God speaks to you through His Word. Ask God to help you understand it. Search God's Word for what He is really telling you, not what you want Him to say.

The third tool is *a listening heart*. If you want to be just like Jesus, work on hearing God's voice. Spend time listening for Him until He tells you His lesson for the day—and then go out and live that lesson.

Read: ISAIAH 28:10

When I was growing up, all of us neighborhood kids would play street football. One kid had a dad with a great arm, and as soon as he'd pull in the driveway from work, we'd start yelling for him to come and play. He'd always ask, "Which team is losing?" Then he'd join that team.

When he joined, the whole game changed. He was confident, strong, and had a plan. He'd say, "Okay, here's what we're going to do." The other side was groaning before we left the huddle. We had a new plan and a new leader. He brought new life to our team.

God does the same thing. In this sinful world, we don't need a new play; we need a new plan. We don't need to trade positions; we need a new player. That player is Jesus.

Read: PSALM 116:6

May 10

Faith is not something that you can trade for. You can't come to God and say, "Okay, I've been nice to fifteen people, obeyed my parents twenty-one times, and done twelve good deeds. I'll trade You all that for one ticket to heaven."

Sounds silly, doesn't it? You can't trade your good works for His salvation. The truth is you can never do *enough* good things to trade your way into heaven.

What *does* get you into heaven? The apostle Paul answered that question: "You have been saved by grace because you believe. You did not save yourselves. It was a gift from God. You cannot brag that you are saved by the work you have done" (Ephesians 2:8–9). Heaven is God's gift to those who *believe* that His grace will get them there.

Read: HEBREWS 10:22

August 21

As a young boy, Jesus already heard the call of God. But what did He do when He left the temple? Start rounding up apostles and preaching sermons and performing miracles? No, He went home with His folks, learned the family business, and finished growing up.

And that is exactly what you should do. Want to bring focus to your life? Do what Jesus did. Be home, love your family, and take care of the business of growing up. "But, Mr. Lucado, I want to be a missionary when I grow up," you might say. Your first mission field is at home. To be able to show love to people overseas, you first need to be able to show love to the people who live across the hall.

Read: COLOSSIANS 3:23

May 11

Just imagine. You are standing before the judgment seat of Christ. The book of your life is opened, and the reading begins—each sin, each lie, each moment of anger and selfishness. But as soon as the sin is read, grace and forgiveness are given.

The result? God's mercy will be heard throughout the universe. For the first time in history, we will understand how great His goodness is. Not just a one-size-fits-all grace. But personal grace. Just for you. Specific kindness. Individual forgiveness. We will stand in awe as one sin after another is read and then forgiven.

The devil will hide. The angels will sing. And we will stand tall in God's grace. As we see how much He has forgiven us, we will see how much He loves us. And we will worship Him.

Read: 2 TIMOTHY 2:19

August 20

Growing a stronger faith should be the goal of every Christian. Maturing is a must.

If you stopped growing taller, your parents would be worried, right? They would try to get help for you.

When a Christian's faith stops growing, help is needed too. If you are the same Christian you were last year, be careful. You might need to get a checkup. Not on your body, but on your heart. Not a physical, but a spiritual.

May I suggest one?

Why don't you check your habits? Make these four habits part of your daily activities, and see what happens.

First, the habit of prayer. Second, the habit of Bible study. Third, the habit of giving both your time and your money to God's work here on earth. And, last, the habit of fellowship and friendship with other Christians.

Read: 2 PETER 3:18

May 12

Camp life is a lot different from home life. At first you love it—You leave your socks on the floor. You don't shower or brush your teeth. You can be a total slob, and no one cares.

Then things start to change. You get tired of stepping over dirty clothes, and you really wish you had a clean bed. And that smell you've been smelling—it's you! Finally, out come the soap and toothpaste, and up go the socks and towels. What happened? You knew there was a better way.

Isn't that what Jesus does for us? Before we knew Jesus, our lives were sloppy and selfish. But suddenly now we want to do good—even when no one is looking! Go back to the old mess? Are you kidding? Not a chance. There's a better way.

Read: PHILIPPIANS 3:14

August 19

Imagine climbing to the top of a mountain. Turn your back on this noisy world and climb up the rocks that God Himself created. Listen to His voice whispering to you in the wind. No crowds. No school. No practice. Just you and God.

God invites you to sit on that high rock, far above the trees, and look out with Him at the ancient mountain peaks that will never be worn down. He asks you to listen as He says:

"The things that are needed for your salvation will always be there for you."

"There is nowhere you can go tomorrow that I haven't already been."

"My truth will always win out over evil."

"The victory—heaven—is yours."

Spend some quiet time in prayer on God's sacred summit, His mountaintop. It's an unchanging place in an ever-changing world.

Read: ISAIAH 58:11

May 13

Jesus turned to His disciples and asked them a question. *The* question. "Who do you say I am?"

He didn't ask, "What do you think about all the miracles I've done?" He asked, "Who do you say I am?"

He didn't ask, "Who do your friends think I am? Or your parents? Or who does the preacher think I am?" Instead He asked a very personal question, "Who do *you* think I am?"

You will be asked some important questions in your life:

What do you want to be when you grow up?

Who will you marry?

Where will you live?

But the greatest, most important question of all these kinds of questions is an anthill compared to the mountain of a question that Jesus asked in Mark 8:29.

Who do you say I am?

Read: MARK 8:29

We are God's idea. We are His. His face. His eyes. His hands. His touch. We are Him. Look deeply into the face of every human being on earth, and you will see His likeness. We are all created in the image of God.

We are—amazingly and incredibly—the body of Christ. And although we may not always act like our Father, there is no greater truth than this: we are His. That cannot change. He loves us with a love that never dies. Nothing can separate us from the love of Christ (see Romans 8:38–39).

Nothing can separate *you* from the love of Christ.

Read: DEUTERONOMY 7:9

Life is like mountain climbing. There are some mountains that you just can't climb on your own. Mountains like wiping away your sins and getting to heaven. Those are mountains that only God can climb. It's not that you aren't welcome to try; it's just that you aren't supposed to fix all your own problems, or run the whole world, or get yourself to heaven.

Oh, some of you think you can just work a little harder and climb a little faster. That may be enough when it comes to making all As or winning a race. But you can't work hard enough or climb fast enough to get over the mountain of your own sins and mistakes. You need God to map out the way, guide your hands and feet, and hold the ropes so that you don't fall.

Read: 2 CORINTHIANS 12:9

August 17

Only a weak, puny god could be bought with gifts and offerings. Only an uncaring god would be impressed with our pain. Only a heartless god would sell salvation to the highest bidders.

And only a great God would do for His children what they can't do for themselves—save them. God gives you His joy when you give yourself up to Him, not when He defeats you. The first step to getting His joy is to ask for His help, to realize that you aren't good enough for heaven.

Those who choose to follow God understand that they can't get to heaven without Him. Those who choose to follow God ask for His forgiveness for all the wrongs they have done.

And because God is so great, He doesn't just forgive them—He calls them His children.

Read: LUKE 1:50

At the moment I don't feel too smart. I just got off the wrong plane at the wrong airport in the wrong city. I went east instead of west and ended up in Texas instead of Colorado. Oops.

Paul said we've all done the same thing. Not with airplanes and airports, but with our lives and with God. He said: "There is no one without sin. None!" (Romans 3:10). "All people have sinned and are not good enough for God's glory" (v. 23).

It's like we are all on the wrong plane. All of us. Boy and girl. Grown-up and child. Every person has taken the wrong turn at some point. And we need help. The wrong answers are selfishness and chasing after fun (Romans 1 and 2). The right answer is Christ Jesus (3:21–26).

Read: ROMANS 1:17

God sees us with the eyes of a Father. He sees our faults, our mistakes, and our imperfections. But He also sees our value, how much we are worth.

What did Jesus know that made Him able to do what He did on the cross?

Here's part of the answer. He knew the value of people. He knew that each human being is a treasure. And because He did, people did not make Him worried and stressed. They made Him joyful.

So when Jesus looks at you, He is able to look past all your faults, your mistakes, and your imperfections. He does not see you as one big mess of stress. You are His source of joy.

Read: 1 SAMUEL 16:7

We all know what it's like to be in a house that's not yours. Maybe you've spent time at a friend's house or grandparent's house. Maybe you've slept in a bunk bed at camp or a hotel room on vacation. They may have food, and they may be warm, but they are not "your father's house"—where your father is. And your true home is where your heavenly Father is.

You may wonder if there is a place here on earth for you. People can make you feel unwanted. You won't always feel welcome here.

You shouldn't. This isn't your home. This language you speak, it's not yours. This body you wear, it isn't the real you. And the world you live in, this isn't home. Where is your real home? Heaven—and it's waiting for you.

Read: JOHN 15:19

August 15

You will live forever in your body—or at least in a perfect version of it. Your body will be different, but you won't have a different body. You will have this one. It will be made new and perfect, but it will be the same one. Does that change your view of your body? I hope so.

God created you, and He loves His creation. You should as well. Respect your body. I did not say worship it, but I did say respect it. The Bible tells us that the human body is the temple of God—the place where the Holy Spirit lives. Be careful how you use it and take care of it. You wouldn't want anyone trashing your home, would you? God doesn't want anyone trashing His either. After all, it is *His* temple, isn't it?

Read: 1 CORINTHIANS 6:19

It's a wonderful day when we stop working *for* God and start working *with* God. For years I thought of God as the boss of a big company—a nice guy, but definitely *The Boss*. And I was just one of His loyal helpers. He had His office, and I had mine. I went out to do His work and then reported back. I could call Him as much as I wanted. He encouraged me and supported me, but I didn't think He went with me. Then I read 2 Corinthians 6:1: "We are workers together with God."

Workers *with* God? Wow! We don't just report back to God. We don't check in with Him and leave; we check in with Him and then follow. We are always in the presence of God.

Every moment is sacred!

Read: 1 CORINTHIANS 3:9

August 14

There are some things we want to do but simply aren't able to. I, for example, would love to sing for others. The problem is, I'm not the best singer, so it would not give the same joy to those listening to me.

Paul gave good advice in Romans 12:3: "Do not think that you are better than you are. You must see yourself as you really are."

In other words, know your strengths. When you help in the nursery, do the toddlers follow you? You may be a teacher. When you offer to serve, do others follow your example? You may be a leader. Where can you do the most for God? Find out your strengths, and then focus on them. Failing to focus there may keep you from doing the thing that God has created you to do.

Read: ROMANS 12:6

May 18

God didn't look at our messed-up, mixed-up lives and say, "I'll die for you when you deserve it."

No, in spite of all our sins, in spite of our not obeying His Word, He chose to adopt us. And for God, there's no going back.

God's grace is a come-as-you-are promise from a one-of-a-kind God. You've been *found*. You've been *called*—His Spirit has touched your heart and made you want to follow Him. And you've been *adopted* by Him.

So trust your Father and claim this verse as your own: "Christ died for us while we were still sinners. In this way God shows His great love for us" (Romans 5:8). You've been adopted by God! "You are God's child, and God will give you what He promised, because you are His child" (Galatians 4:7).

Read: MATTHEW 9:12-13

Ask yourself two questions:

Is there any sin in my life that I haven't confessed to God?
Confession is telling God you did what He saw you do. He doesn't need to hear it—He already knows. He also knows you need to say it. Whether you think it's too small to be mentioned or too big to be forgiven doesn't matter. Your job is to be honest with God.

Are there any worries in my heart that I haven't given to God?

"Give all your worries to Him, because He cares for you" (1 Peter 5:7). The German word for *worry* means "to strangle." The Greek word means "to divide the mind." Worry is like a noose around your neck that won't let you breathe. Worry confuses your mind. Neither of these things will lead you to God's joy.

Read: PSALM 32:3

The question is not simply, "Who can be against us?" You could answer that one. Who is against you? The bully in gym class, the mean girl, sickness, sadness, tiredness, loneliness—and all those other "ness-es" that make messes in our lives.

If Paul's question were only "Who can be against us?" we could list our enemies. It would be easier for us to simply list them than to fight them. But that is not the question. The question is, "If God is for us, who can be against us?"

God *is* for you. A bully may have picked on you, your teachers may have overlooked you, your brothers and sisters may not speak to you, but within earshot of your prayers is the One who made the oceans—God! He is for you, and He fights for you!

Read: ROMANS 8:31

August 12

God is often more patient and more forgiving with us than we are with ourselves. We may believe that if we mess up—if we sin—then we aren't truly saved. If we struggle and stumble, then we aren't really His children. We are supposed to be "made new" when we belong to Christ (2 Corinthians 5:17). So if we sometimes still fall back to our old selfish ways, then we might think, *Uh-oh. Maybe I wasn't made new after all.*

If you are worried about these things, please remember that "God began doing a good work in you. And he will continue it until it is finished when Jesus Christ comes again" (Philippians 1:6).

In other words, don't worry. God's still working on you.

Read: ROMANS 5:4-5

May 20

Many people don't understand God's anger. They confuse the anger of God with the anger of people. But the two are very different. People's anger is usually selfish. It shows itself in explosions of temper and violence. We get upset because we've been ignored, skipped over, or cheated. When we don't get what we want, we get mad. This is the anger of people. It is not, however, the anger of God.

God doesn't get angry because He doesn't get His way. He gets angry because we disobey Him. And He knows that by disobeying Him, we will always end up getting hurt. After all, what kind of father sits by and watches his child hurt himself? Not God!

Read: COLOSSIANS 3:5-6

Do you ever think God is too small to do the big things we ask of Him? Do you ever think your problem is just too enormous, even for God? Do you ever think to yourself: *There's no way out of this mess. This problem is just too big.*

If you've had thoughts like that, listen to what His Word says: "With God's power working in us, God can do much, much more than anything we can ask or think of " (Ephesians 3:20).

Did you get that? You can't even *begin* to imagine what God will do for you and through you—when you let His power work in you. When your problems seem bigger than the answers, ask your big God to help. Keep praying and trusting Him with everything in your life. See what He will do!

Read: ISAIAH 40:29

What a thought! Your name is written on God's hand. Your name is on God's lips. Maybe you've seen your name in some special places. On an award or a trophy. But to think that your name is on God's hand and on God's lips... Wow! Could it be?

Or maybe you have never had your name honored. Maybe you've never made the honor roll. Or won the trophy. Or been chosen for the team. If so, it may be even harder for you to believe that God knows your name.

But He does. It's written on His hand. Spoken by His mouth. Whispered by His lips. *Your name.*

Read: ISAIAH 4:16

August 10

Pay attention to the prayers of a Christian parent. Pay attention to the power that comes when a parent asks God to be with or help a child. Who knows what prayers will be answered in your life ten or twenty years from now because of your parents' faithful prayers right now? God listens to thoughtful parents.

And God listens to thoughtful children. Just as your parents pray for you, take time to pray for your parents. They are God's children too. They need His help, His guidance, His wisdom just as much as you do. There is nothing more special, more precious than the time that a child spends struggling with prayers to God. Your prayers are heard—and answered—in heaven.

Read: ISAIAH 54:13

God lives forever. He has no beginning and no end. But He knows the beginning and end of everyone who has ever lived. He knows every moment of their lives. And He knows the answer to their every question.

"How long am I going to be without a friend?"

"How long am I going to be sick?"

"How long am I going to struggle to get along with my family?"

Do you really want God to answer? He could, you know. He could answer exactly how many weeks, or days, or hours. But God doesn't usually do that. He asks us to trust Him. He uses our times of loneliness, sickness, and struggle to teach us to turn to Him for help. Although our troubles sometimes seem to last forever, they really don't—but heaven does. So hold on.

Read: 1 CHRONICLES 29:15

The Bible says that after Jesus calmed the storm, "those who were in the boat worshiped Jesus and said, 'Truly You are the Son of God!' " (Matthew 14:33).

After the storm, the disciples worshiped Him. As far as we know, they had never, as a group, done that before. Check it out. Open your Bible. Search for a time when the disciples joined together and praised Jesus. You won't find them worshiping when He healed the leper. Reached out to the woman at the well. Preached to the masses. They were willing to follow. Willing to leave family. Willing to cast out demons. Willing to be in the Lord's army.

But only after Jesus stilled the storm on the sea did they worship Him. Why?

Simple. This time they knew *they* were the ones who had been saved.

Read: MATTHEW 8:25-26

May 23

"All people will know that you are My followers if you love each other" (John 13:35). Stop and think about this verse for a minute. Could it be that *unity*—loving one another and sticking together—is the way we can tell the world about Jesus?

If unity is the key to reaching others, shouldn't we, as Paul said, "do all [we] can to continue together" (Ephesians 4:3)? If unity is important in heaven, then shouldn't it be important on earth?

If God's people want to help others learn about Jesus, we must first show them that we love each other. That means we don't talk badly about each other. We treat each other with kindness and respect. We help each other, and we stick together. God's people must love each other *before* they can love others.

Read: 2 THESSALONIANS 3:5

August 8

"When Jesus was raised from the dead it was a signal"—a signal that He had defeated death! Don't you just love that verse?

The resurrection of Jesus is like an exploding signal flare shot into the sky. It tells all of us who are truly searching for Christ that it is safe to believe. Safe to believe in eternal justice. Safe to believe in eternal life. Safe to believe in heaven as our home and the earth as its front porch. Safe to believe in a time when questions and worries won't keep us awake. Safe to believe in a time when pain and sickness won't keep us down. Safe to believe in endless days and real praise.

Because we can believe the resurrection story, it is safe to believe the rest of God's story.

Read: ROMANS 6:9-10

If we confess our sins..." The biggest word in the Bible just might be that tiny two-letter one *if*. Admitting we have messed up is exactly what we often don't want to do.

"Me? A sinner? Oh sure, I get in a little trouble once in a while, but I'm a pretty good kid."

"Hey, I'm just as good as Amy, and I'm definitely better than Jake."

Pretty good. Just as good. Better than. Sound familiar? We all say these things. We compare ourselves to others, and we look good. But in heaven, pretty good just isn't good enough.

When you get to the point of being sorry for your sins, when you admit that Jesus is your only choice, then confess. Tell Him about your sins, and give all your cares to Him. He is waiting for you.

Read: 1 JOHN 1:9

The single most difficult goal is to have truth *and* love. Love by itself is a difficult goal to reach. Especially *agape* love—the kind of love that wants the best for others.

Truth is a tough one too. Not the who-really-broke-the-glass kind of truth. But the kind of truth that wants to lead others to God.

But try to have truth and love at the same time, and—whew!—you've got your work cut out for you.

Love in truth. Truth in love. Never one without the other. You can't just accept what someone believes if it doesn't match the truth of the Bible. Sometimes you *do* need to help others see what God's Word really says. But it's important to help for the right reason—because you love them—and not just because you want to be right.

Read: PSALM 89:14

May 25

During the early days of the Civil War, a Union soldier was arrested for sneaking away and leaving the army. He was sentenced to die, but his plea for mercy found its way to the desk of President Abraham Lincoln.

The president felt sorry for the soldier and signed a pardon. The soldier returned to service, fought the rest of the war, and was killed in the last battle. After his death, the signed letter from the president was found inside his shirt pocket.

Close to the heart of the soldier were his leader's words of pardon. The soldier found courage in the grace of the president. But we have an even greater pardon from an even greater Leader—the pardon of all our sins from our heavenly King. Let God's grace give you the courage to do the right thing.

Read: 1 TIMOTHY 1:16

You can change the way you look on the outside with money and clothes and stuff, but changing *who* you are—changing your heart—that's an *inside* job.

Sin is when we do what we know is wrong. It is disobeying our Creator. And because God is perfect and has no sin in Him, He cannot be around us when we have sin inside us. Our sin keeps us from getting close to God.

But—and here's the really great news—God loves us so much that He doesn't want to be cut off from us. So He gave us a way to get rid of the sin inside us. He gave us His Son. When we choose to follow Jesus, He washes away all our sins. Jesus changes us from the *inside* out.

Read: ROMANS 12:2

The Bible is not just a collection of made-up fairy tales. These are actual moments in history when a real God helped real people in real pain so we could answer the question, "Where is God when I hurt?"

How does God react to broken dreams? Read the story of Jairus and his dying daughter (Luke 8:40–56). How does God feel about those who are sick? Picture yourself at the pool of Bethesda as He heals the crippled man (John 5:1–9). Do you wish God would speak to your lonely heart? Then listen as He speaks to the disciples on the road to Emmaus (Luke 24:13–35).

He's not doing it just for them. He's doing it for you and me. He still comes into your world. He comes to do what you can't.

Read: PSALM 34:18

When we choose to follow God's plans, we can trust our wants and desires. Our life's mission—our purpose—is found at the place where God's plan and our pleasures meet. *What do you love to do? What makes you happy?* God will use those things in His plan for your life.

Some people feel a need to help the poor. Others enjoy leading at church. Each of us has been made to serve God in our own special way.

The things you enjoy doing are no accidents. They are important messages. They shouldn't be ignored; they should be respected. Just as the wind turns the direction of the weather vane, so God uses the things you love to do to turn the direction of your life. God is too kind to ask you to do something you hate.

Read: PSALM 37:4

May 27

Jesus didn't act unless He saw His Father act. He didn't judge until He heard His Father judge. He never did or said anything without His Father's guidance.

Because Jesus could hear what others couldn't—His Father's voice—He acted differently than they did. Do you remember in the Bible when everyone was troubled about the man born blind? Jesus wasn't. He knew that the blindness would reveal God's power (John 9:3). Remember the time when everyone was upset about Lazarus's illness and death? Jesus wasn't. It was as if Jesus could hear the thoughts of His Father telling Him that Lazarus would live.

Do you think the Father wants the same kind of hearing for us? Yes! God wants the same closeness with you that He had with His Son. All it takes is spending time with Him.

Read: PSALM 42:1

August 4

Have you ever seen the way a groom looks at his bride during the wedding? I have. Perhaps it's because as the minister at the wedding, I'm standing right next to the groom.

If the light is just right, I can see a tiny reflection in his eyes. Her reflection. The sight of her reminds him why he's here. His jaw softens. His smile becomes real again. He forgets he's wearing a tux. When he sees her, any thought of running away becomes a joke. It's written all over his face, "I can't live without my bride!"

Those are the exact same feelings Jesus has. Look into His eyes, and you will see the reflection of someone clothed in pure grace.

Who is this person Jesus is waiting for? *It's you*! You are the joy of God's heart.

Read: ISAIAH 62:5

God is not finished with you yet. Oh, you may think He is. You may think you're right where you need to be. You may think you've got life all figured out.

If so, think again. You've still got a lot of growing to do.

"God began doing a good work in you. And He will continue it until it is finished when Jesus Christ comes again" (Philippians 1:6).

Did you see what God is doing? *A good work in you.* Did you see when He will be finished? *When Jesus comes again.* Let me make God's message clear for you: *God ain't finished with you yet.*

Read: 1 CORINTHIANS 1:8

Anger and hate make our blood pump faster and our hearts race. As time goes by, we need more and more anger and hate to keep our blood pumping faster.

There is a dangerous point at which anger stops being an emotion and becomes the reason we do what we do—and what we do is usually the wrong thing. A person who only cares about getting even moves further and further away from being able to forgive. And that moves him further and further away from God.

Hatred is like a rabid dog that turns and bites its owner. Revenge is like a raging fire that burns up the one who set it. Anger is like a trap that catches the hunter.

And mercy is the choice that can set them all free.

Read: ROMANS 12:1

There are those who say hell is not real. But if you take punishment out of the Bible, then you also take away God's justice. It's as if you're saying that God doesn't care if people sin, and that He doesn't care about those who have been hurt by others. But God says, "I am the One who punishes" (Romans 12:19).

And if everyone gets into heaven, then why did God send Jesus to wash away our sins? Jesus Himself said, "The only way to the Father is through Me" (John 14:6).

If we say there is no punishment for those who refuse to follow Jesus, then we're saying that the Bible is a lie. Because over and over the Bible tells us that some will be lost and some will be saved (for example, Matthew 25:33). We *must* choose to follow Jesus to be saved.

Read: DANIEL 12:2

August 2

It's hard to see things grow old. The town in which I grew up is growing old. Some of the buildings are boarded up or torn down. The movie theater where I went with my friends has "For Sale" up on its sign.

I wish I could make it all new again. I wish I could blow the dust off the streets, but I can't.

Just like I can't dust the sin off my soul or erase my mistakes. But God can. "He restores my soul," wrote the shepherd. God doesn't change our souls. He *restores* them. He doesn't just cover up the old; He makes the old new. The Master Builder pulls out the original plan and makes it just like new. He restores the liveliness. He restores the energy. He restores the hope. He restores your soul.

Read: PSALM 23:3

Matthew wrote that Jesus "healed those who were sick." Not some, not just the good people, not the deserving. But "those who were sick."

Surely, among them, there were a few people who didn't deserve good health. The same God who gave Jesus the power to heal also gave Him the power to see into people's hearts. I wonder if Jesus was ever tempted to say to the liar, "Get out of here, buddy."

And Jesus could not only see their past, but He could also see their future. There were surely those in the crowds who would use their new health to hurt others. Jesus healed tongues that might someday curse; eyes that could covet; hands that could kill.

Each time Jesus healed, He had to overlook what He knew. Something that He still does today—for us.

Read: MATTHEW 14:14

August 1

Satisfied? That is one thing we are not. We take the vacation of our dreams. We enjoy every kind of fun in the sun. But we are not even on the way home before we dread the end of the trip and begin wishing for the next one.

We are not happy. We are not satisfied.

As a kid we say, "If only I were a teenager." As a teen we say, "If only I were an adult." As an adult, "If only I were married." As a married person, "If only I had kids."

Why is it so hard to be content?

Because there's nothing on earth that can satisfy our deepest want—to see God. Everything in His creation is whispering that we will see Him, and we won't be content until we do.

Read: 1 TIMOTHY 6:7-8

May 31

Antonio Stradivari was a violin maker in the 1700s. He once said that to make a violin less than his best would be to rob God, who could not make Antonio Stradivari's violins without Antonio.

He was right. God could not make Stradivarius violins without Antonio Stradivari. Certain gifts were given to that craftsman that no other violin maker possessed.

In the same way, there are things you can do that no one else can. Perhaps it's encouraging your friends, playing basketball, or drawing the beauty of God's creation. There are things that only *you* can do, and you were put here by God to do them. Pretend that life is an orchestra and you have been given an instrument and a song. You owe it to God to play them both the very best that you can.

Read: PSALM 139:14

July 31

Jesus made a promise to us: "I will come back." And when He returns, it will be a frightening time for people who didn't follow Jesus. They will be judged by the One they refused to worship. But children of God do not need to be afraid because Jesus has promised to take us home to heaven with Him.

But can we believe Jesus' promise? How can we know He will do what He said? How can we believe He will save us and set us free from our sins? How can we know He will come back?

Because He's already come back once. Because the stone was rolled away and His tomb was empty. Because Jesus lives.

Read: 1 CORINTHIANS 15:23

June 1

Everyone likes to be invited—to a friend's house, a party, a club. But the best invitations of all don't come from friends. They come from God.

Our God is an inviting God. He invited Mary to birth His Son, the disciples to fish for men, the woman caught in sin to start over, and Thomas to touch His wounds.

In fact, it seems His favorite word is *come*.

"*Come*, we will talk these things over. Your sins are red like deep red cloth. But they can be as white as snow" (Isaiah 1:18).

"All you who are thirsty, *come* and drink" (Isaiah 55:1).

"*Come* to Me, all of you who are tired and have heavy loads. I will give you rest" (Matthew 11:28).

God invites and reaches out. God is reaching out to you.

Read: MATTHEW 4:19

July 30

Jesus tells us to do two things. First, "Love the Lord your God with all your heart, soul and mind." And, second, "Love your neighbor as you love yourself" (Matthew 22:37–39).

Let's take a look at that second command. Who is your neighbor? Everyone around you. That's the part of the verse that most people talk about. But they don't usually talk about the second part: "as you love yourself."

Jesus wasn't talking about an "I'm-better-than-you" kind of love. He's talking about loving yourself because you are an amazing creation of God. You have to love yourself and know how you want to be treated *before* you can know how to love your neighbor.

When you don't love yourself, it's easier for others to be unkind to you. So, love your neighbor... as *you love yourself.*

Read: MATTHEW 11:30

A branch is connected to a vine. It's impossible to tell where the branch starts and the vine ends. The branch lives on the vine and gets its strength from the vine.

That's the kind of relationship God wants with you. God doesn't want you to turn to Him only when you need something or when something is wrong. God wants your thoughts and your heart to be with Him always.

If a branch is cut off the vine, it begins to dry up. In the same way, when you are cut off from God, your heart begins to dry up. You have lost the source of your life. Stay connected to the vine—to God—and He will keep you strong.

Read: JOHN 15:4

July 29

Could you use some courage? Jesus understands when you do. After all, He chased the butterflies out of the stomachs of His nervous disciples.

We need to remember that the disciples were ordinary men given an extraordinary task. Long before they were pictured in the stained-glass windows of our churches, they were trying to make a living and raise a family. They didn't come from a long line of priests, and they weren't superheroes. But they loved Jesus more than they were afraid, and because of that, they did some extraordinary things.

When you choose to follow Jesus, He will take care of your earthly fears. He will help you to be brave. Remember, Jesus gave courage and strength to His disciples, and He'll give it to you too.

Read: ISAIAH 41:13

June 3

Peek into the prison and see Paul for yourself: bent over and frail, chained to the arm of a Roman guard. He's alone. No family. No property. He can't see well and he's worn out. Doesn't look like a hero, does he?

Doesn't sound like one either. He called himself the worst sinner in history. He was a Christian-killer before he was a Christian leader. At times his heart was so heavy, Paul's pen dragged itself across the page. "What a miserable man I am! Who will save me from this body that brings me death?" (Romans 7:24).

Only heaven knows how long Paul stared at that question before he found the courage to write, "I thank [God] for saving me through Jesus Christ our Lord!" (Romans 7:25).

Yes, look and see this true hero of faith.

Read: PHILIPPIANS 4:12

Before His crucifixion on the cross, Jesus told His disciples that He would be leaving them. "Where I am going you cannot follow now. But you will follow later" (John 13:36).

That left the disciples with some questions. Peter asked, "Lord, why can't I follow you now?" (John 13:37).

Jesus' answer was as tender as a parent answering a child. "Don't let your hearts be troubled. Trust in God. And trust in Me. There are many rooms in my Father's house. I would not tell you this if it were not true. I am going there to prepare a place for you.... I will come back. Then I will take you to be with Me so that you may be where I am" (John 14:1–3).

In other words, "You trust in Me, and I'll take care of you."

Read: JEREMIAH 17:7

June 4

Power comes in many forms.

The boy who refuses to be kind to his sister.

The teacher who plays favorites with grades and praise.

The popular kid who gives the silent treatment to anyone who doesn't follow the crowd.

It might be the taking of someone's turn, or it might be the taking of someone's life.

But they are all spelled the same: P-O-W-E-R. They all have the same goal: "I will get what I want."

And they all have the same end: uselessness. It's useless. Absolute power is not possible. When you make it to the top, the only way left to go is down.

A thousand years from now, will it matter what the world thought of you? No, but it will make a difference what God thought of you. And that's what really matters.

Read: 1 CORINTHIANS 3:19

One of Jesus' greatest skills was His ability to stay focused. His life never got distracted. He kept heading in the right direction.

As Jesus looked out at His future, He had many choices. He could have been a success at any of them. He could have fought the Romans to free the Jewish people. He could have been happy as a teacher in the temple and educated the people. But in the end He chose to be a Savior and save souls.

Anyone who was with Him for any length of time heard it from Jesus Himself: "The Son of Man came to find lost people and save them" (Luke 19:10). The heart of Jesus was focused on just one thing. The day He left the carpentry shop of Nazareth He had one goal—the cross.

Read: MARK 10:45

Let there be..."

With those three words, history began. Time began. "Let there be..." light. And "let there be..." day and night, sky and earth. And then on this earth the mighty hand of God went to work.

He carved out the canyons and dug the deepest oceans. He made mountains burst out of the flatlands. He flung the stars into the sky and made the universe sparkle with His light.

Do you want to see God's might? Look at the mountains. Want to see His gentleness? Touch His wildflowers. Want to hear His power? Listen to the thunder.

Today you will come face-to-face with God's creation. When you see the beauty of nature all around you, let it remind you to give thanks to God for the world He made.

Read: COLOSSIANS 1:16

What is *unity*? Unity is choosing to get along. And though it may sound simple, it isn't always easy to do.

What does having unity mean?

It means thinking about what others want and need—not just what you want and need.

It means that when someone makes you angry, you choose to let that anger go.

It means that when someone hurts your feelings, you don't hurt them back.

It means forgiving when you don't want to. It means being kind when you would rather not.

It means being patient when you want to be mad.

Unity means sticking together when the selfish ways of this world want to pull you apart. Doesn't unity sound like one of God's great ideas?

Read: COLOSSIANS 3:13

Growing up can be dangerous. It's like hiking on a rocky trail with lots of chances to trip and fall. The devil would love to knock you down or get you lost. So it's smart to be prepared.

As you grow up, you'll start making more and more decisions for yourself. You'll face some tough choices. And you'll have to decide which way your life will go and which way it won't. But God doesn't leave you on your own. "I made you and will take care of you," He promises.

Look in His Word; He gives you plenty of advice. And look around you; He gives you plenty of good examples to follow.

The choices that you make now will prepare you for the choices you must make as a grown-up. And they all start with choosing God.

Read: ISAIAH 46:4

Do you want to know who God is? Just look up at the night sky and see what He has done. Do you want to know His power? Take a look at His creation. Are you curious about His strength? Pay a visit to His home address:

1 Billion Starry Sky Avenue

God is perfect and all-powerful. He is not touched by even a hint of sin, not limited by time, not weakened by tiredness.

Is an eagle bothered by a bump in the road? No, he rises above it. Is the whale troubled by the hurricane? Of course not! He dives beneath it. Is the lion irritated by the mouse standing in his way? No, he steps over it.

How much more is God able to rise above, dive beneath, and step over the troubles of the earth!

Read: MATTHEW 19:26

June 7

We will all face tough times. Even as kids, some of you already have. Maybe you've been made fun of and made to feel that you didn't fit in. Maybe you've had to move or had friends who moved away. Maybe those around you don't understand your faith. Maybe you've even lost someone you love.

Hard days can leave you feeling tired and all alone. They can make you just want to give up. But don't.

When you're having a tough day, God can seem far away, and getting to Him can seem like an impossible journey. But it isn't. Let me cheer you on and give you hope. God never said the journey would be easy. But He did say that if you trust in Him, He will get you home to heaven.

Read: 2 CORINTHIANS 4:18

July 24

Praise. *Honor. Glorify.* What do all these words really mean? Well, these are all just fancy words that mean telling God how wonderful He is. Telling Him that you know He is all-powerful. Telling Him how grateful you are for all that He does. And simply telling Him how very much you love Him.

We were created to praise, honor, and glorify God. But how do we *do* that? There are many different ways. You can praise God with the songs you sing. You can honor Him with your gifts of time and service and money. You can glorify Him by helping others. But that's not all. Pray to Him. Study Him. Notice His work in nature. There are so many different ways to praise God.

But the most important thing is simply to praise Him—each and every day.

Read: 1 TIMOTHY 1:17

John the Baptist would never get hired as a preacher today. What would the people think? "His clothes are 'made from camel's hair' (Mark 1:6)! He 'ate locusts and wild honey' (Mark 1:6)! I'm not sitting next to him!"

John's message was simple: confess your sins and turn away from them because the Lord is on His way (Matthew 3:2). John set himself apart to tell others about Jesus. Everything about him focused on that one task. His dress. His food. His words. His actions.

You don't have to be like the world to make a difference. You don't have to be like the crowd to change it. You don't have to lower yourself down to their level to lift them up to God's level.

Holiness doesn't try to fit in. Holiness tries to be like God.

Read: JAMES 4:4

July 23

On the first day of school, most teachers will give you a list of classroom rules. Rules that help the school day go much more smoothly. It's good to have some rules for the other parts of your life too. Here are some God-given, time-tested rules for life that will make all your days go much more smoothly :

- Love God more than anything else.
- Live like someone is watching even when no one is.
- Do your best, at home and away from home.
- Obey your parents.
- Be kind and respectful to everyone.
- Don't spend money that you don't have yet.
- Pray twice as much as you think you need to.
- Forgive yourself because God has forgiven you.
- Remember that God always loves you...*always*.

Read: ECCLESIASTES 12:13

June 9

How *could a loving God punish people for all eternity*? People often ask that question. But we need to get a couple of things straight.

First, *God* does not choose to punish people. God tells us what will happen if we don't obey His Word, and then He lets *us* choose. If we don't follow His Word, then we choose to be punished. But if we choose to obey, then He rewards us with heaven. God simply respects our choice.

Second, God punishes *sinners*, not *people*. He punishes those who have chosen to do wrong.

And, last, God offers a way for *everyone* to get to heaven. All we have to do is believe in His Son and obey His Word. But God won't force us to believe—it has to be our choice.

Read: ISAIAH 53:6

July 22

It's easy to look at the world around you and say, "If only I could make the team... If only I could be popular... If only I had the right clothes... If only we had more money... If only my family were different..."

I believe God has an "if only" list too. His list probably goes something like this: "If only he knew how much I love him... If only she would ask for My help... If only he would trust Me... If only she would let Me save her...."

There are a lot of "if only" things that you can't do anything about. But you can choose to do something about God's "if only" list. You can choose to believe in Him and to obey His Word—and you can make God's "if onlys" come true.

Read: GALATIANS 4:7

I love short sentences. Below are some of my favorite short sentences. Keep the ones you like. Forget the ones you don't. Share them when you can.

- Pray all the time. You don't even have to use words!
- God forgets the past. Be like Him.
- I've often been sorry for being greedy. But for giving? Never.
- Don't ask God to do what you want. Ask God to help you do what is right.
- No one is useless to God. No one.
- Nails didn't hold Jesus on the cross. Love did.
- You will never forgive anyone more than God has already forgiven you.

Read: MATTHEW 6:7

July 21

How far do you want God to go to get your attention? If God has to choose between your eternity in heaven and your happiness on earth, which do you hope He chooses?

What if God moved you to another land? (As He did Abraham.) What if you were kidnapped, made a slave, and then thrown into prison. (Remember Joseph?) How about being struck blind on the side of the road like Paul was?

God does whatever it takes to get our attention. Isn't that the message of the Bible? God's never-ending, all-out pursuit of us. God on the hunt. God in the search. Peeking under the bed for hiding kids, searching in the classrooms and on the practice fields for those who are lost. Looking for you because He wants you with Him forever.

Read: JOEL 2:13

Worry makes you forget who's in charge. And when you focus on yourself, you become anxious about many things. You worry that:

Your parents won't understand.

Your classmates will make fun of you.

You won't ever be as gifted as your friends are.

You won't ever make a difference.

Worry makes you think about the things *you* want rather than the things *God* wants for you. You become more interested in what others think than what God thinks. You may even find yourself jealous of a friend's gifts and doubting God's plan.

God has given you talents. He has done the same for your friend. If you focus on your friend's talents, you won't see your own. But if you focus on the gifts that God has given to *you*, you could inspire both yourself and your friend.

Read: 1 PETER 5:7

What will it be like to finally see Jesus face-to-face? How will it feel?

I believe it will be greater than anything we could ever imagine. But I like to imagine anyway. And I imagine it will be better than Christmas morning, better than a birthday, better than an ice-cream sundae—all rolled into one!

When we see Jesus face-to-face, we will be looking into the eyes of One who loves us more than anyone else ever could. And His love will fill us with complete joy and peace.

All our sins and mistakes will be washed away forever. There will be no more guilt, shame, loneliness, or being left out. We will never mess up, stumble, or doubt again. Why? Because "when Christ comes again, we will be like him" (1 John 3:2).

And I can't wait!

Read: 1 CORINTHIANS 13:12

June 12

Healthy families love each other. They are kind, tender, and honest with each other. As we spend time with our families, we become like them. God designed our homes to be the place where we can always go to find love.

The same is true in our relationship with God. Sometimes we go to Him with our joys, and sometimes with our hurts. But we always go, and we always find His love. And the more we go, the more we become like Him. Paul said, "This change in us brings more and more glory" (2 Corinthians 3:18).

As we grow closer to God, we begin to sound like Him and think more like Him. And hopefully our hearts begin to look more like His every day.

Read: EPHESIANS 4:23-24

Some time ago my daughter Andrea got a splinter in her finger. I took her to get the first aid kit. I set out some tweezers, ointment, and a Band-Aid.

She didn't like what she saw. "I just want the Band-Aid, Daddy."

Sometimes we are just like Andrea. We come to Jesus with our sins, but all we want is for them to be covered up. We want to skip the treatment. We want to hide our sin. And one has to wonder if God—even in His great mercy—will heal what we just try to hide.

How can God heal what we say isn't even there? How can God touch what we cover up? Tell God all about your messes. Your sins. Your mistakes. He can fix them—and He won't even need a Band-Aid.

Read: 1 JOHN 1:8

In the book of Revelation, John said that the city of heaven is like "a bride dressed for her husband."

How can a city be like a bride? Well, even though you're a long way from being a bride or a groom, you've seen brides, haven't you? Is there anything more beautiful than a bride?

Maybe it is her beautiful dress or the way her eyes sparkle like diamonds. Or maybe it's the blush of love that colors her cheeks or the flowers that she carries in her arms.

A bride. She is like a beautiful promise, saying to her groom, "I'll be with you forever."

Heaven, too, is a beautiful promise. It is God's promised reward for His children. Heaven is your promised home.

Read: REVELATION 21:2

July 18

Imagine the pool of Bethesda. In Bible times, it was the place where the hopelessly sick came (John 5:1–9). It was, they believed, their last chance to be healed. For at a certain time, an angel would stir the waters. Whoever stepped in first, after the waters were stirred, would be healed.

But imagine all those who weren't healed. Imagine walking by the pool. The ground must have looked like a battlefield covered with wounded bodies.

As people passed by, they heard an endless wave of groans and saw a field of faceless needs. Most just walked past. But not Jesus. The people needed Him, so He was there.

Little did they know that this was God—walking slowly, stepping carefully between the beggars and the blind. Because wherever His hurting children are, that is where God is.

Read: MATTHEW 8:17

June 14

Corrie ten Boom was a Dutch Christian who helped Jews escape the Nazis. She used to say, "When the train goes through a tunnel and the world gets dark, do you jump out? Of course not. You sit still and trust the engineer to get you through."

God is still in control. It's not over until He says so. Life's troubles and trials are a reason to sit still and trust the Great Engineer to get us through.

What do you do when you're facing a tough time? Go back and read the story of God. Let Him remind you that you aren't the first person to be sad or to need help. Let God remind you of how He helps His children.

Read the story of God and remember that its message is for you!

Read: JEREMIAH 32:27

When I was seven years old, I ran away. I'd had enough of my father's rules. With my clothes in a paper bag, I stormed out and marched down the alley. But I didn't go far. I got to the end of the alley and realized I was hungry, so I went back home.

Although my disobedience was brief, it was still disobedience. And if you had stopped me in that alley, I might have said, "I don't need a father. I'm too big for his rules."

I didn't hear the rooster crow, like Peter. Or the fish belch, like Jonah. I didn't get a robe, like the prodigal son. But I learned from my earthly father what they learned from their heavenly Father: I can count on God to be on my side no matter what. You can too.

Read: DEUTERONOMY 31:8

June 15

God's invitation to us is clear. It's simple. God is clear about what He asks of us—to obey Him—and clear about what He offers—to live with Him in heaven forever. But whether or not we say yes to His invitation is our choice.

Isn't it incredible that God leaves the choice to us? Think about it. There are many things in life we can't choose. We can't, for example, choose our family. We can't choose the weather. We can't choose whether or not we are born with a big nose or blue eyes or curly hair. We can't even choose how people act toward us.

But we can choose where we spend eternity. The big choice God leaves to us. The most important choice is ours.

And it's the only choice that really matters.

Read: JOSHUA 24:15

To whom does God offer His gift of grace and forgiveness? To the smartest? The most beautiful or the funniest? No. His gift is for us all—rich and poor, popular and unpopular, sports stars and science geeks. All God's children.

And God wants each of us so badly that He'll take us no matter what shape we're in. He wants us "as is"—with all our mistakes, worries and fears, and imperfections.

God isn't about to wait for us to be perfect before He saves us. (He knows we'll *never* be perfect!) Do you think He's waiting until we are no longer tempted to sin? Not hardly. Remember, Jesus died for us *while* we were still sinners. His sacrifice—and our salvation—does not depend on what we do. It depends on who God is.

Read: ROMANS 11:6

June 16

Only God's grace can save us. Not what we do. Not our talents. Not our feelings. Not our strength.

Like Paul on the road to Damascus, we need to know that we are sinners, and we need a savior.

And like Peter when he stepped out of the boat and onto the stormy water, we need to know that we are going down, and Jesus is still standing up. We need to reach out for Jesus' hand and hold on to His grace that saves us.

Grace is when God steps in and fills our lives with His peaceful presence. We hear His voice, saying, "Don't be afraid. It is I" (John 6:20). He wants us to let go of our past and hold on to Him.

Amazingly, when we do, all our failures are forgiven.

Read: ROMANS 3:23-24

July 15

Faith is trusting what our eyes can't see.

- Human eyes see the prowling lions. Daniel's faith sees the angel close the lions' mouths.
- Human eyes see storms. Noah's faith sees the rainbow.
- Human eyes see a giant. David's faith sees the giant Goliath fall.
- Your eyes see your faults. Your faith sees Jesus your Savior.

When you look in the mirror, do you see your mistakes, your sins? It's easy for our human eyes to only see what is wrong. We need to use our "eyes of faith"—the way God sees things—to see what is right. Look in the mirror again, using your eyes of faith. I can tell you what God sees there—His beloved child, the one He has promised all of heaven to.

Read: HEBREWS 11:1

Anger. It's loud. It's loud in your heart. It's loud in your mind. And the louder it gets, the more desperate we become.

Some of you are thinking, *You don't have any idea how hard my life is.* You're right. I don't know how tough your life is right now. But I have a very clear idea of how miserable your future will be if you don't deal with your anger.

Anger is like a dark thundercloud: black, threatening, and terrible. It's like a storm in your heart that is threatening to turn into a tornado. You can't change what other people do, but you can change how you act toward them. You can't always help being angry, but you can control what you do with your anger.

Ask God to help you—because He will.

Read: PSALM 37:8

You aren't an accident or something that just happened. You are a gift to the world, a divine work of art signed by God.

One of the greatest gifts I ever received is a football signed by thirty former professional quarterbacks. There is nothing unique or special about the ball itself. What makes it special are the signatures.

The same is true with us. If you look at all of nature, *Homo sapiens* (people) are not unique. We aren't the only creatures with flesh and hair and blood and hearts. What makes us special is the signature of God on our lives. We are His works of art. We are created in His image. We are important and valuable, not because of what we do but because of whose we are.

Read: JEREMIAH 1:5

Seems to me that God gives us a lot more grace than we could ever imagine.

Seems to me that we could do the same for others.

You know that you're not perfect. That's what God's grace is for—it washes away all those times that you're not perfect.

When God gives you His grace, He then asks you to do something for Him: *remember that no one else is perfect either.* Give a little grace to those around you.

Because it's going to happen. Your brother or sister will say something mean. Your best friend will hurt your feelings. Once in a while your mom or dad might snap at you. When those things happen, don't hold a grudge. Forgive them, and give a little grace—because God has given you a whole lot.

Read: MATTHEW 18:21-22

The key to knowing God's heart is having a relationship with Him. A *personal* relationship. God will speak to you differently than He will speak to others.

Just because God spoke to Moses through a burning bush doesn't mean we should all sit next to a bush and wait. God used a fish to get Jonah's attention. Does that mean we should have worship services at Sea World? No. God reveals His heart personally—in a different way—to each person.

That is why the time you spend with God is so important. You can't know His heart just by having a quick chat once in a while or a weekly visit. You learn God's will as you spend time with Him every single day.

Hang out with God long enough, and you will come to know His heart.

Read: JOHN 6:40

How do you make God a part of your day, all day long? How do you know when His unseen hand is on your shoulder and His whispering voice is in your ear? How can you learn to hear and know the voice of God? Here are a few ideas:

Give God your waking-up thoughts. Before you face the day, face the Father. Before you step out of bed, pray that God will guide your steps this day.

Give God your waiting thoughts. Spend time with Him being still and quiet. Wait to hear His voice.

Give God your whispering thoughts. Just imagine: every moment is a chance to talk to God.

Give God your end-of-day thoughts. As you settle into bed, let your mind settle on Him. End the day as you started it—talking to God.

Read: EPHESIANS 6:18

July 12

Have you ever heard the word *repent*? Christians use that word a lot, but what does it really mean? *Repent* means more than just saying we're sorry. *Repent* means we stop doing what is wrong and we try to do what is right. It is turning away from selfishness and sin and turning to God. It's like a spiritual U-turn.

When we repent, the sadness we feel on the *inside* shows itself in the way we act on the *outside*.

You look at the love of God and compare it to your sins. You can't believe He loves you like He does—with all your mess-ups and mix-ups. And knowing this makes you want to change the way you live. That is what it means to repent.

Read: ROMANS 2:4

John the Baptist was in prison, and he was beginning to doubt. Why wasn't Jesus coming to save him? So he sent Jesus a question: "Are you the one who was to come, or should we expect someone else?" (Matthew 11:3 NIV).

Jesus didn't scold John for his doubt. Instead, Jesus said, "Go back to John and tell him about the things you hear and see: The blind can see. The crippled can walk…. And the Good News is told to the poor" (Matthew 11:4–5).

Now John understood. It wasn't that Jesus was silent. John had just been listening for an answer to his *earthly* problems. But Jesus was busy taking care of John's *heavenly* problem—a way into heaven. Remember that the next time you think God hasn't answered your prayers.

Read: MATTHEW 7:7

Exactly what is *praise*? I like King David's definition: "Tell the greatness of the Lord with me. Let us praise His name together" (Psalm 34:3).

Praise is telling the Lord how great He is. It is *magnifying* Him. That is, praise is making our view of God—His power, His might, and His majesty—bigger. Growing our understanding of Him. Like stepping into the cockpit of creation to see where God the Pilot sits and how He works. As we draw nearer, He seems larger. And isn't a *big* view of God what we need? Don't we have *big* challenges, *big* worries, *big* questions? Of course. So we need a big view of God.

Praise gives us that. When we sing words such as "holy, holy, holy," they help us focus on how big and wonderful God really is.

Read: REVELATION 4:8

Let's imagine God standing on the porch of heaven. He's waiting for you, hoping, searching the horizon for a glimpse of His child. You're the one God is looking for.

God is the waiting Father, the caring Shepherd in search of His lost lamb. His legs are scratched, His feet are sore, and His eyes are burning. He climbs the cliffs and crosses the fields. He cups His hand to His mouth and calls down into the canyon.

And the name He calls is yours.

God doesn't just sit up in heaven and hope that you'll come looking for Him. He comes looking for you. There is nowhere you can go that He cannot find you. He wants to save you. He is calling out your name—*your* name. All you have to do is answer Him.

Read: EZEKIEL 34:11

Dig deep enough in every heart and you'll find it: the wish to understand why God created you. As surely as you breathe, you will someday wonder, "Why am I here? Why did God make me?"

Some people search for the answer in their work. These people believe that who they are is what they *do*, so they do a lot.

For other people, who they are is what they *have*. Others try to have all the fun they possibly can, and still others try to be the sports star or the movie star.

But none of these things are the right answer to the question "Why am I here?" We only have one purpose in life. One reason for being here. To praise God.

So shouldn't we do just that?

Read: MATTHEW 22:37

June 22

Every so often a storm will come along, and I'll look up into the dark sky and say, "God, a little light, please?"

That's probably what the disciples were asking as the storm tossed their boat around the sea. And the light did come for the disciples. A figure came to them walking on the water. It wasn't what they expected. They weren't looking for Jesus to come walking on the water!

And because Jesus came in a way they didn't expect, they almost missed seeing the answer to their prayers.

And unless we look and listen closely, we risk making the same mistake. Just like real thunderstorms, sometimes our lives become stormy, and bad things happen. But God's lights in our dark storms are as bright as the stars—if only we'll look for them.

Read: MATTHEW 14:25–26

July 9

To those who believe that Jesus is our Savior, He has promised a new birth into a new life with God. It's a life free of shame and full of the hope of heaven. Does that mean that your old, sinful side will never show its ugly head again? Or that you'll never be tempted to do wrong again?

To answer that question, compare your new birth in Jesus to a newborn baby. It takes time for a baby to grow and learn. But in the hospital delivery room, is the parent ashamed of the baby? Is the mom embarrassed that the baby can't spell... or walk... or stand up and give a speech? Of course not. The parents aren't ashamed; they're proud. They know the baby will grow and learn with time. God knows you will grow and learn too.

Read: 2 PETER 3:9

It's important to know that no friendship is perfect, no family is perfect, no person is perfect. And you're not perfect. So when you decide to make a relationship work— to get along—you have to remember that people will still make mistakes, get on your nerves sometimes, or hurt your feelings.

So how do you get along with others? Look at what God says in Romans 12:10-18: "Give your brothers and sisters more honor than you want for yourselves.... Wish good for those who do bad things to you.... Be happy with those who are happy. Be sad with those who are sad.... If someone does wrong to you, do not pay him back by doing wrong to him.... Do your best to live in peace with everyone."

In other words... *choose to love.*

Read: 1 THESSALONIANS 5:15

July 8

Imagine you've traveled back to Bible times, to talk to a man on death row. He is Jewish by birth. A tentmaker. An apostle of Christ. His name is Paul. You wonder what it is that keeps this man going as he nears his death. So you ask him some questions.

Do you have family, Paul? *No.*

How is your health? *My body has been beaten, and I am tired.*

Have you gotten any awards? *Not on earth.*

No awards. No family. What do you have that matters, Paul? *My faith in Jesus. It's all I have. But it's all I need. I have kept the faith.*

Paul leans back against the wall of his cell and smiles. He smiles because he knows God's promise: "If you are faithful, I will give you the crown of life" (Revelation 2:10).

Read: 1 TIMOTHY 1:19

June 24

Revelation 21 describes heaven like this: "Shining with the glory of God" (v. 11). "Made of pure gold" (v. 18). "Each gate was made from a single pearl. The street of the city was made of pure gold" (v. 21). "There is no night there" (v. 25). Now look at the description of hell: it is a "lake of fire that burns with sulfur" (Revelation 19:20).

We all have to spend eternity somewhere—either heaven or hell. And when we choose God, His *mercy* saves us from hell, and His *grace* blesses us with heaven.

All the people who don't know God will spend an eternity somewhere too. Knowing that should make us want to pray, serve, and reach out to those who don't know Him. Helping others choose heaven is the most important mission we'll ever have.

Read: MATTHEW 28:19

The storm at sea was terrible. The wind howled. The waves beat against the boat. And the disciples battled for their lives. They were already frightened. So when they saw Jesus walking toward them on the water, they called him a ghost. To them, the glow was anything but God.

When we see gentle lights in the middle of the storms of life, we often think the same thing. We see the kindness, the helping hand, the answer. But we think they are just an accident or good luck. We think they're anything but God.

But when you're in the middle of a bad day or problem, God uses the people around you to help. That friendly hug, offer to help, or unexpected answer just when you needed it aren't accidents. They are God. He's closer than you think.

Read: MATTHEW 14:27

June 25

Jesus had a definition for greed. He called it "measuring who you are by what you have."

The result of this kind of thinking is easy to guess: If you are what you own, then by all means own it all! No price is too high. Go ahead, gossip to be popular. Lie to get the new shoes. Steal to get the new game. If you *have* more, then you'll *be* more—more important, more popular, more happy. Right?

Not right. Greed costs a lot. Gossip will cost you friendships. Lies and stealing will cost you the trust of your family. And all of those things will pull you away from God.

When you believe that you are what you own, you actually lose the things that are truly important—friends, family, and faith. And nothing is worth that.

Read: LUKE 12:15

When we see Jesus, what will we see? The perfect Priest.

In Bible times, a priest was the one who presented people to God and God to people. Revelation says that, in heaven, Jesus "was dressed in a long robe. He had a gold band around His chest" (1:13). That's the type of robe and gold band that only priests used to wear.

You have known other priests. They may or may not have been church leaders, but they were all people who wanted to bring you to God. But even these people needed a priest. "Jesus is the kind of high priest that we need. He is holy; He has no sin in Him. He is pure and not influenced by sinners. And He is raised above the heavens" (Hebrews 7:26).

Jesus is the perfect Priest.

Read: 2 THESSALONIANS 1:10

Living a Christian life is like climbing a great wall. The wall is high, and the risk is higher. You take your first step up the day you confess Jesus as the Son of God. He gives you His safety harness—the Holy Spirit. He hands you a rope—His Word.

As the climb goes, you become tired. You become afraid. You lose your focus. You lose your grip. You do that thing you know you shouldn't do. And for a moment, you fall. Tumbling wildly. Dizzy. Out of control.

But then the rope tightens. You hang there in the safety harness and find that it's strong. You trust the rope to hold you up. And although you can't see your Guide, you know Him—Jesus. He is strong. And He is able to keep you from falling.

Read: JUDE 24

Bitterness is hurt and anger that you hold on to. It is that wish for revenge against those who have wronged you. And it is its own prison.

The walls of this prison are slippery with hatred. Puddles of muddy anger darken the floor. The stench of betrayal fills the air and stings the eyes. A cloud of self-pity blocks out the light.

Bitterness can trap you when you've been lied to, betrayed by friends, or bullied by enemies. It will trap you when you choose to hold on to the hurt. When you choose not to forgive. When you choose to hate. Bitterness will trap your heart in a prison.

But you can escape it. How? Choose to let go of the hurt, to forgive. Choose to accept God's love and grace, and then give it to others.

Read: MATTHEW 6:14

Did you know that worship changes your face?

That's exactly what happened to Jesus on the mountain. His face was changed, and it "became bright like the sun" (Matthew 17:2).

When we worship, our face becomes filled with the light and love of God.

The link between the face and worship is no accident. Our face is the most seen part of our bodies. It is covered less than any other part. It is also the way people know who we are. We don't fill a school yearbook with pictures of people's feet. We fill it with pictures of faces. God wants to take our faces—the most seen and easily remembered part of us—and use them like a mirror to reflect His goodness.

Take some time to worship God today, and let Him change your face.

Read: 2 CORINTHIANS 3:18

July 4

Punishment is easy for me to understand. *You break the rules, and you pay the price*. But God's grace? That's not as easy to understand. *You break the rules, but Jesus pays the price*. Want examples?

• David the psalmist became David the murderer, but by God's grace, he became David the psalmist again.

• Peter denied Jesus three times before he preached Jesus.

• Zacchaeus was a crook. He stole money, and his heart was dirty with greed. But Jesus still had time for him.

• The thief on the cross was headed for hell and hung out to die one minute, but he was heaven-bound and smiling the next.

Story after story. Prayer after prayer. It seems that God is looking more for ways to get us home to heaven than for ways to keep us out.

Read: JOB 10:12

What do you do when people mistreat you or those you love? Do flames of hate burn your heart? Does your face burn red and hot?

Or do you reach up to Jesus? Do you ask Him to help you control the angry fire? Do you pull out a bucket of mercy—and throw it on the angry flames? Do you put out the fire?

Don't get on the roller coaster of anger. Be the one who says, "Yes, he treated me wrong, but I am going to be like Christ. I'll be the one who says, 'Father, forgive them. They don't know what they are doing' " (Luke 23:34).

If Jesus could look down from the cross and say those words, then so can you. Ask Him to help you put out the fire.

Read: 1 PETER 2:20

July 3

God wants to spend time with us so that He can change our face. And He wants to change our face so that it shows His glory.

God loves to change the faces of His children. He rubs away the wrinkles of worry and fear. Shadows of shame become smiles of grace. He softens clenched jaws and gritted teeth. He smooths away lines of anger. His touch gives rest to weary eyes, and tears of sadness become tears of peace and relief.

How does God do that? Through worship and praise. You'd think it would be harder, wouldn't you? Maybe spending forty days without food like Moses did and Jesus did. Or memorizing the entire book of Leviticus. But no. God's plan is simpler. When we praise Him and worship Him, He changes our faces and fills them with joy.

Read: PSALM 40:3

June 29

Some people will try to get you to go a different way. A way that doesn't include God. Those people may be on TV or singing the songs you listen to. They may be sitting right next to you at the lunch table. They'll tell you to swap your honesty for a good grade on a test, or that it's okay to wear clothes that show too much. They'll tell you it's okay to make fun of others if it makes you look good. They will even tell you it's okay to turn away from God in order to be more popular.

When people tempt and tease you to do wrong, remember what God says: "Be careful. Continue strong in the faith… and be strong" (1 Corinthians 16:13). God will give you the strength to stand strong.

Read: 1 PETER 1:15

July 2

Imagine if you thought of every second of every day as a chance to talk to God.

By the time your life is over, you will have spent six months waiting at stoplights, a year and a half looking for lost stuff, and a whopping five years standing in lines.

Why don't you give these "lost" moments to God? By giving God your thoughts, the ordinary becomes extraordinary.

Prayers can simply be silent whispers—just between you and God. Simple prayers—such as "Thank You, Father," "Be with me this day, God," and "I trust You, Jesus"—can turn a car ride into worship. You don't need a special place. Just pray where you are. Let the kitchen become a church and the classroom become a chapel. Give God your whispering thoughts.

Read: PSALM 139:23

When do we have salvation?

When we look to Jesus and believe that He is our Savior. Read the great promise of John 3:16: "For God loved the world so much that He gave His only Son. God gave His Son so that whoever believes in Him may not be lost, but have eternal life." That is *your* promise from God.

Wow! What a promise! Salvation. New life. All just for following Jesus. But even though God's plan is so simple, there are still those who don't trust His promise.

That's where you come in. Show the world the joy and hope that come from following Him. Show people that His power to help and to save the world is real. And show them that He wants to save them too.

Read: JOHN 3:36

July 1

Some of you are still arguing, whining and complaining. You're complaining to your parents, to the teacher, to friends, to anyone who will listen. Every chance you get, you're going over those same hurt feelings again and again.

I have one question for you: Who made you God? I don't mean to sound like a smart aleck, but why are you doing His work for Him?

"I will punish those who do wrong," God declared. "I will repay them" (Hebrews 10:30).

Judging people is God's job—not yours. To think something else is to think that God can't do it.

Revenge is unholy. To forgive someone is to show them God's holiness. Forgiveness is not saying that the one who hurt you was right. Forgiveness is saying that you know God is faithful and *He* will do what is right.

Read: PROVERBS 20:22